The READ Through the Bible

IN A YEAR **MAP**

FOR WOMEN

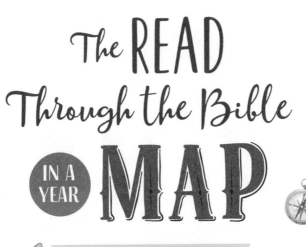

The READ Through the Bible
IN A YEAR MAP

FOR WOMEN

BARBOUR BOOKS
An Imprint of Barbour Publishing, Inc.

Published by Barbour Books, an imprint of Barbour Publishing, Inc., 1810 Barbour Drive, Uhrichsville, Ohio 44683, www.barbourbooks.com

Our mission is to inspire the world with the life-changing message of the Bible.

 Member of the
Evangelical Christian
Publishers Association

Printed in China.

A Start-to-Finish MAP to Guide You THROUGH GOD'S WORD

Does God really care if I read the Bible?

Does His Word really apply to my life?

And is it even possible to read through the entire Bible?

The answer is. . .*YES!*

Discover the secret to a flourishing faith as you spend time in the amazing, unchanging Word of God!

This creative journal will guide you through the entire Bible in one year—as you write out specific prayers and important takeaways from your daily Bible reading. For 365 days, you'll encounter a start-to-finish, comprehensive reading plan that includes an Old Testament, New Testament, and Psalms or Proverbs reading for each day. (Read in the Bible version of your choice!) Be sure to write the date on each of your daily Bible reading maps, so you can look back and track your progress as you work your way through the scriptures.

This daily Bible reading map will not only encourage you to dig deep into God's Word. . .it will also help you to make daily scripture reading a habit—*for life!*

DAY 1

Today's Date: _____

📍 MY PRAYER FOR TODAY: ....
....
....

READ:

GENESIS 1;
MATTHEW 1;
PSALM 1

MY TAKEAWAY FROM TODAY'S BIBLE READING:
....
....
....

And God saw every thing that he had made,
and, behold, it was very good.
GENESIS 1:31

DAY 2

Today's Date: _____

📍 MY PRAYER FOR TODAY: ....
....
....

MY TAKEAWAY FROM TODAY'S BIBLE READING:
....
....
....

READ:

GENESIS 2–4;
MATTHEW 2;
PSALM 2

Yet have I set my king upon my holy hill of Zion.
I will declare the decree: the LORD hath said unto me,
Thou art my Son; this day have I begotten thee.
PSALM 2:6–7

Today's Date: _____

📍 MY PRAYER FOR TODAY: ....
....
....

MY TAKEAWAY FROM TODAY'S BIBLE READING:
....

READ:

GENESIS 5–7;
MATTHEW 3;
PSALM 3

....
....

Repent ye: for the kingdom of heaven is at hand.
MATTHEW 3:2

Today's Date: _____

📍 MY PRAYER FOR TODAY: ....
....
....

READ:

GENESIS 8–10;
MATTHEW 4;
PSALM 4

MY TAKEAWAY FROM TODAY'S BIBLE READING:
....
....
....

I will both lay me down in peace, and sleep: for thou,
LORD, only makest me dwell in safety.
PSALM 4:8

DAY 5

Today's Date: _____

📍 MY PRAYER FOR TODAY: ....
....
....

READ:

Genesis 11–13;
Matthew 5:1–20;
Psalm 5

MY TAKEAWAY FROM TODAY'S BIBLE READING:
....
....
....

*My voice shalt thou hear in the morning, O Lord; in the
morning will I direct my prayer unto thee, and will look up.*
Psalm 5:3

DAY 6

Today's Date: _____

📍 MY PRAYER FOR TODAY: ....
....
....

MY TAKEAWAY FROM TODAY'S BIBLE READING:
....
....
....

READ:

Genesis 14–16;
Matthew 5:21–48;
Psalm 6

*Love your enemies, bless them that curse you,
do good to them that hate you, and pray for them
which despitefully use you, and persecute you.*
Matthew 5:44

Today's Date: _____

MY PRAYER FOR TODAY: ....
....
....

MY TAKEAWAY FROM TODAY'S BIBLE READING:
....
....
....

READ:

GENESIS 17–18;
MATTHEW 6:1–18;
PSALM 7

*When thou prayest, enter into thy closet, and when thou hast shut
thy door, pray to thy Father which is in secret; and thy Father
which seeth in secret shall reward thee openly.*
MATTHEW 6:6

Today's Date: _____

MY PRAYER FOR TODAY: ....
....
....

READ:

GENESIS 19–20;
MATTHEW 6:19–34;
PSALM 8

MY TAKEAWAY FROM TODAY'S BIBLE READING:
....
....
....

*When I consider thy heavens, the work of thy fingers, the moon and the
stars, which thou hast ordained; what is man, that thou art mindful of
him? and the son of man, that thou visitest him?*
PSALM 8:3–4

DAY 9

Today's Date: _____

📍 MY PRAYER FOR TODAY: ....
....
....

READ:

Genesis 21–23;
Matthew 7:1–11;
Psalm 9:1–8

MY TAKEAWAY FROM TODAY'S BIBLE READING:
....
....
....

Ask, and it shall be given you; seek, and ye shall find; knock, and it shall be opened unto you: for every one that asketh receiveth; and he that seeketh findeth; and to him that knocketh it shall be opened.
MATTHEW 7:7–8

DAY 10

Today's Date: _____

📍 MY PRAYER FOR TODAY: ....
....
....

MY TAKEAWAY FROM TODAY'S BIBLE READING:
....
....
....

READ:

Genesis 24;
Matthew 7:12–29;
Psalm 9:9–20

And they that know thy name will put their trust in thee: for thou, LORD, hast not forsaken them that seek thee.
PSALM 9:10

Today's Date: _____

MY PRAYER FOR TODAY: ....
....
....

MY TAKEAWAY FROM TODAY'S BIBLE READING:
....
....
....

READ:

GENESIS 25–26;
MATTHEW 8:1–17;
PSALM 10:1–11

*I will make thy seed to multiply as the stars of heaven,
and will give unto thy seed all these countries; and in thy
seed shall all the nations of the earth be blessed.*
GENESIS 26:4

Today's Date: _____

MY PRAYER FOR TODAY: ....
....
....

READ:

GENESIS 27:1–28:9;
MATTHEW 8:18–34;
PSALM 10:12–18

MY TAKEAWAY FROM TODAY'S BIBLE READING:
....
....
....

Arise, O LORD; O God, lift up thine hand: forget not the humble.
PSALM 10:12

DAY 13

Today's Date: _____

📍 MY PRAYER FOR TODAY: ....
....
....

READ:

Genesis 28:10–29:35;
Matthew 9;
Psalm 11

MY TAKEAWAY FROM TODAY'S BIBLE READING:
....
....
....

For the righteous LORD loveth righteousness;
his countenance doth behold the upright.
PSALM 11:7

DAY 14

Today's Date: _____

📍 MY PRAYER FOR TODAY: ....
....
....

MY TAKEAWAY FROM TODAY'S BIBLE READING:
....
....
....

READ:

Genesis 30:1–31:21;
Matthew 10:1–15;
Psalm 12

The words of the LORD are pure words:
as silver tried in a furnace of earth, purified seven times.
PSALM 12:6

Today's Date: _____

DAY 15

📍 MY PRAYER FOR TODAY: ....
....
....

MY TAKEAWAY FROM TODAY'S BIBLE READING:
....
....
....

READ:

GENESIS 31:22–32:21;
MATTHEW 10:16–36;
PSALM 13

But I have trusted in thy mercy; my heart shall rejoice in thy salvation.
I will sing unto the LORD, because he hath dealt bountifully with me.
PSALM 13:5–6

Today's Date: _____

DAY 16

📍 MY PRAYER FOR TODAY: ....
....
....

READ

GENESIS 32:22–34:31;
MATTHEW 10:37–11:6;
PSALM 14

MY TAKEAWAY FROM TODAY'S BIBLE READING:
....
....
....

Blessed is he, whosoever shall not be offended in me.
MATTHEW 11:6

DAY 17 Today's Date: _____

📍 MY PRAYER FOR TODAY: ....
....
....

READ:

Genesis 35–36;
Matthew 11:7–24;
Psalm 15

MY TAKEAWAY FROM TODAY'S BIBLE READING:

....
....
....

He that hath ears to hear, let him hear.
MATTHEW 11:15

DAY 18 Today's Date: _____

📍 MY PRAYER FOR TODAY: ....
....
....

MY TAKEAWAY FROM TODAY'S BIBLE READING:

....
....
....

READ:

Genesis 37–38;
Matthew 11:25–30;
Psalm 16

*Thou wilt shew me the path of life: in thy presence is fulness
of joy; at thy right hand there are pleasures for evermore.*
PSALM 16:11

Today's Date: _____

MY PRAYER FOR TODAY: ....
....
....

MY TAKEAWAY FROM TODAY'S BIBLE READING:

READ:

GENESIS 39–40;
MATTHEW 12:1–29;
PSALM 17

....
....
....

Keep me as the apple of the eye,
hide me under the shadow of thy wings.
PSALM 17:8

Today's Date: _____

MY PRAYER FOR TODAY: ....
....
....

READ:

GENESIS 41;
MATTHEW 12:30–50;
PSALM 18:1–15

MY TAKEAWAY FROM TODAY'S BIBLE READING:

....
....
....

For whosoever shall do the will of my Father which is in heaven,
the same is my brother, and sister, and mother.
MATTHEW 12:50

DAY 21   Today's Date: _____

📍 MY PRAYER FOR TODAY: ....
....
....

READ:

Genesis 42–43;
Matthew 13:1–9;
Psalm 18:16–29

MY TAKEAWAY FROM TODAY'S BIBLE READING:
....
....
....

For thou wilt light my candle: the Lord
my God will enlighten my darkness.
Psalm 18:28

DAY 22   Today's Date: _____

📍 MY PRAYER FOR TODAY: ....
....
....

MY TAKEAWAY FROM TODAY'S BIBLE READING:
....
....
....

READ:

Genesis 44–45;
Matthew 13:10–23;
Psalm 18:30–50

As for God, his way is perfect: the word of the Lord
is tried: he is a buckler to all those that trust in him.
Psalm 18:30

Today's Date: _____

MY PRAYER FOR TODAY: ....
....
....

MY TAKEAWAY FROM TODAY'S BIBLE READING:
....
....
....

READ:

GENESIS 46:1–47:26;
MATTHEW 13:24–43;
PSALM 19

*Let the words of my mouth, and the meditation of my heart,
be acceptable in thy sight, O LORD, my strength, and my redeemer.*
PSALM 19:14

Today's Date: _____

MY PRAYER FOR TODAY: ....
....
....

READ

GENESIS 47:27–49:28;
MATTHEW 13:44–58;
PSALM 20

MY TAKEAWAY FROM TODAY'S BIBLE READING:
....
....
....

*Now know I that the LORD saveth his anointed; he will hear him
from his holy heaven with the saving strength of his right hand.*
PSALM 20:6

DAY 25

Today's Date: _____

📍 MY PRAYER FOR TODAY: ....
....
....

READ:

Genesis 49:29–
Exodus 1;
Matthew 14;
Psalm 21

MY TAKEAWAY FROM TODAY'S BIBLE READING:
....
....
....

Be thou exalted, Lord, in thine own strength:
so will we sing and praise thy power.
Psalm 21:13

DAY 26

Today's Date: _____

📍 MY PRAYER FOR TODAY: ....
....
....

MY TAKEAWAY FROM TODAY'S BIBLE READING:
....
....
....

READ:

Exodus 2–3;
Matthew 15:1–28;
Psalm 22:1–21

But be not thou far from me, O Lord:
O my strength, haste thee to help me.
Psalm 22:19

Today's Date: _____

MY PRAYER FOR TODAY: ....
....
....

MY TAKEAWAY FROM TODAY'S BIBLE READING:
....
....
....

READ:
Exodus 4:1–5:21;
Matthew 15:29–
16:12;
Psalm 22:22–31

For the kingdom is the LORD's:
and he is the governor among the nations.
PSALM 22:28

Today's Date: _____

MY PRAYER FOR TODAY: ....
....
....

READ:

Exodus 5:22–7:24;
Matthew 16:13–28;
Psalm 23

MY TAKEAWAY FROM TODAY'S BIBLE READING:
....
....
....

If any man will come after me, let him deny himself, and take up
his cross, and follow me. For whosoever will save his life shall lose it:
and whosoever will lose his life for my sake shall find it.
MATTHEW 16:24–25

DAY 29

Today's Date: _____

📍 MY PRAYER FOR TODAY: ....
....
....

READ:

Exodus 7:25–9:35;
Matthew 17:1–9;
Psalm 24

MY TAKEAWAY FROM TODAY'S BIBLE READING:
....
....
....

The earth is the LORD's, and the fulness thereof;
the world, and they that dwell therein.
PSALM 24:1

DAY 30

Today's Date: _____

📍 MY PRAYER FOR TODAY: ....
....
....

MY TAKEAWAY FROM TODAY'S BIBLE READING:
....
....
....

READ:

Exodus 10–11;
Matthew 17:10–27;
Psalm 25

Unto thee, O LORD, do I lift up my soul.
PSALM 25:1

Today's Date: _____

📍 MY PRAYER FOR TODAY: ....
....
....

MY TAKEAWAY FROM TODAY'S BIBLE READING:
....

....

....

READ:

Exodus 12;
Matthew 18:1–20;
Psalm 26

Judge me, O Lord; for I have walked in mine integrity:
I have trusted also in the Lord; therefore I shall not slide.
Psalm 26:1

Today's Date: _____

📍 MY PRAYER FOR TODAY: ....
....
....

READ:

Exodus 13–14;
Matthew 18:21–35;
Psalm 27

MY TAKEAWAY FROM TODAY'S BIBLE READING:
....

....

....

Peter. . .said, Lord, how oft shall my brother sin against me,
and I forgive him? till seven times? Jesus saith unto him, I say not
unto thee, Until seven times: but, Until seventy times seven.
Matthew 18:21–22

DAY 33

Today's Date: _____

📍 MY PRAYER FOR TODAY: ....
....
....

READ:

Exodus 15–16;
Matthew 19:1–15;
Psalm 28

MY TAKEAWAY FROM TODAY'S BIBLE READING:
....
....
....

*The LORD is my strength and my shield; my heart trusted
in him, and I am helped: therefore my heart greatly
rejoiceth; and with my song will I praise him.*
PSALM 28:7

DAY 34

Today's Date: _____

📍 MY PRAYER FOR TODAY: ....
....
....

MY TAKEAWAY FROM TODAY'S BIBLE READING:
....
....
....

READ:

Exodus 17–19;
Matthew 19:16–30;
Psalm 29

*Jesus said unto him, If thou wilt be perfect, go and sell
that thou hast, and give to the poor, and thou shalt
have treasure in heaven: and come and follow me.*
MATTHEW 19:21

Today's Date: _____   **DAY 35**

○ MY PRAYER FOR TODAY: ....
....
....

MY TAKEAWAY FROM TODAY'S BIBLE READING:

READ:

Exodus 20–21;
Matthew 20:1–19;
Psalm 30

....
....
....

*Thou hast turned for me my mourning into dancing: thou
hast put off my sackcloth, and girded me with gladness. . . .
O Lord my God, I will give thanks unto thee for ever.*
Psalm 30:11–12

Today's Date: _____   **DAY 36**

○ MY PRAYER FOR TODAY: ....
....
....

READ:

Exodus 22–23;
Matthew 20:20–34;
Psalm 31:1–8

MY TAKEAWAY FROM TODAY'S BIBLE READING:

....
....
....

*Into thine hand I commit my spirit:
thou hast redeemed me, O Lord God of truth.*
Psalm 31:5

DAY 37

Today's Date: _____

📍 MY PRAYER FOR TODAY: ....

....

....

READ:

Exodus 24–25;
Matthew 21:1–27;
Psalm 31:9–18

MY TAKEAWAY FROM TODAY'S BIBLE READING:

....

....

....

But I trusted in thee, O Lord:
I said, Thou art my God.
PSALM 31:14

DAY 38

Today's Date: _____

📍 MY PRAYER FOR TODAY: ....

....

....

MY TAKEAWAY FROM TODAY'S BIBLE READING:

....

....

....

READ:

Exodus 26–27;
Matthew 21:28–46;
Psalm 31:19–24

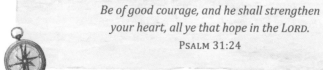

Be of good courage, and he shall strengthen
your heart, all ye that hope in the Lord.
PSALM 31:24

Today's Date: _____ **DAY 39**

📍 MY PRAYER FOR TODAY: ....
....
....

MY TAKEAWAY FROM TODAY'S BIBLE READING:
....

....

....

> **READ:**
>
> Exodus 28;
> Matthew 22;
> Psalm 32

Many sorrows shall be to the wicked: but he that trusteth in the Lord, mercy shall compass him about.
Psalm 32:10

Today's Date: _____ **DAY 40**

📍 MY PRAYER FOR TODAY: ....
....
....

> **READ:**
>
> Exodus 29;
> Matthew 23:1–36;
> Psalm 33:1–12

MY TAKEAWAY FROM TODAY'S BIBLE READING:
....

....

....

Rejoice in the Lord, O ye righteous: for praise is comely for the upright.
Psalm 33:1

DAY 41

Today's Date: _____

📍 MY PRAYER FOR TODAY: ....

....

....

READ:

Exodus 30–31;
Matthew 23:37–
24:28;
Psalm 33:13–22

MY TAKEAWAY FROM TODAY'S BIBLE READING:

....

....

....

Our soul waiteth for the Lord:
he is our help and our shield.
Psalm 33:20

DAY 42

Today's Date: _____

📍 MY PRAYER FOR TODAY: ....

....

....

MY TAKEAWAY FROM TODAY'S BIBLE READING:

....

....

....

READ:

Exodus 32–33;
Matthew 24:29–51;
Psalm 34:1–7

O magnify the Lord with me,
and let us exalt his name together.
Psalm 34:3

Today's Date: _____

MY PRAYER FOR TODAY:..................................
....
....

MY TAKEAWAY FROM TODAY'S BIBLE READING:

....
....
....

READ:

Exodus 34:1–35:29;
Matthew 25:1–13;
Psalm 34:8–22

*Watch therefore, for ye know neither the day
nor the hour wherein the Son of man cometh.*
Matthew 25:13

Today's Date: _____

MY PRAYER FOR TODAY:..................................
....
....

READ:

Exodus 35:30–37:29;
Matthew 25:14–30;
Psalm 35:1–8

MY TAKEAWAY FROM TODAY'S BIBLE READING:

....
....
....

*And he hath filled him with the spirit of God,
in wisdom, in understanding, and in knowledge,
and in all manner of workmanship.*
Exodus 35:31

DAY 45

Today's Date: _____

📍 MY PRAYER FOR TODAY: ....
....
....

READ:

Exodus 38–39;
Matthew 25:31–46;
Psalm 35:9–17

MY TAKEAWAY FROM TODAY'S BIBLE READING:
....
....
....

*And the King shall answer and say unto them, Verily I say
unto you, Inasmuch as ye have done it unto one of the
least of these my brethren, ye have done it unto me.*
MATTHEW 25:40

DAY 46

Today's Date: _____

📍 MY PRAYER FOR TODAY: ....
....
....

MY TAKEAWAY FROM TODAY'S BIBLE READING:

READ:

Exodus 40;
Matthew 26:1–35;
Psalm 35:18–28

....
....
....

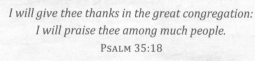

*I will give thee thanks in the great congregation:
I will praise thee among much people.*
PSALM 35:18

Today's Date: _____

MY PRAYER FOR TODAY:..
....
....

MY TAKEAWAY FROM TODAY'S BIBLE READING:

READ:

LEVITICUS 1–3;
MATTHEW 26:36–68;
PSALM 36:1–6

....
....
....

> *Thy mercy, O LORD, is in the heavens;*
> *and thy faithfulness reacheth unto the clouds.*
> PSALM 36:5

Today's Date: _____

MY PRAYER FOR TODAY: ....
....
....

READ:

LEVITICUS 4:1–5:13;
MATTHEW 26:69–
27:26;
PSALM 36:7–12

MY TAKEAWAY FROM TODAY'S BIBLE READING:

....
....
....

> *How excellent is thy lovingkindness, O God! therefore the children*
> *of men put their trust under the shadow of thy wings.*
> PSALM 36:7

DAY 49

Today's Date: _____

📍 MY PRAYER FOR TODAY: ....
....
....

READ:

Leviticus 5:14–7:21;
Matthew 27:27–50;
Psalm 37:1–6

MY TAKEAWAY FROM TODAY'S BIBLE READING:
....
....
....

Delight thyself also in the Lord:
and he shall give thee the desires of thine heart.
Psalm 37:4

DAY 50

Today's Date: _____

📍 MY PRAYER FOR TODAY: ....
....
....

MY TAKEAWAY FROM TODAY'S BIBLE READING:

READ:

Leviticus 7:22–8:36;
Matthew 27:51–66;
Psalm 37:7–26

....
....
....

The steps of a good man are ordered by the Lord: and he
delighteth in his way. Though he fall, he shall not be utterly
cast down: for the Lord upholdeth him with his hand.
Psalm 37:23–24

Today's Date: _____ **DAY 51**

📍 MY PRAYER FOR TODAY: ....
....
....

MY TAKEAWAY FROM TODAY'S BIBLE READING:

....

....

....

> **READ:**
>
> Leviticus 9–10;
> Matthew 28;
> Psalm 37:27–40

Go ye therefore, and teach all nations, baptizing them in the name
of the Father, and of the Son, and of the Holy Ghost. . .and, lo,
I am with you always, even unto the end of the world. Amen.
MATTHEW 28:19–20

Today's Date: _____ **DAY 52**

📍 MY PRAYER FOR TODAY: ....
....
....

> **READ:**
>
> Leviticus 11–12;
> Mark 1:1–28;
> Psalm 38

MY TAKEAWAY FROM TODAY'S BIBLE READING:

....

....

....

For in thee, O LORD, do I hope:
thou wilt hear, O Lord my God.
PSALM 38:15

Today's Date: _____

📍 MY PRAYER FOR TODAY: ....
....
....

READ:

Leviticus 13;
Mark 1:29–39;
Psalm 39

MY TAKEAWAY FROM TODAY'S BIBLE READING:
....
....
....

And now, Lord, what wait I for?
my hope is in thee.
Psalm 39:7

Today's Date: _____

📍 MY PRAYER FOR TODAY: ....
....
....

MY TAKEAWAY FROM TODAY'S BIBLE READING:

READ:

Leviticus 14;
Mark 1:40–2:12;
Psalm 40:1–8

....
....
....

Many, O Lord my God, are thy wonderful
works which thou hast done.
Psalm 40:5

Today's Date: _____

MY PRAYER FOR TODAY: ....
....
....

MY TAKEAWAY FROM TODAY'S BIBLE READING:
....
....
....

READ:

LEVITICUS 15;
MARK 2:13–3:35;
PSALM 40:9–17

*[Jesus] saith unto them, They that are whole have no
need of the physician, but they that are sick: I came not
to call the righteous, but sinners to repentance.*
MARK 2:17

Today's Date: _____

DAY 56

MY PRAYER FOR TODAY: ....
....
....

READ:

LEVITICUS 16–17;
MARK 4:1–20;
PSALM 41:1–4

MY TAKEAWAY FROM TODAY'S BIBLE READING:
....
....
....

*Blessed is he that considereth the poor:
the LORD will deliver him in time of trouble.*
PSALM 41:1

DAY 57   Today's Date: _____

MY PRAYER FOR TODAY: ....
....
....

READ:

Leviticus 18–19;
Mark 4:21–41;
Psalm 41:5–13

MY TAKEAWAY FROM TODAY'S BIBLE READING:
....
....
....

*And [Jesus] arose, and rebuked the wind, and said unto the sea,
Peace, be still. And the wind ceased, and there was a great calm.*
Mark 4:39

DAY 58   Today's Date: _____

MY PRAYER FOR TODAY: ....
....
....

MY TAKEAWAY FROM TODAY'S BIBLE READING:
....
....
....

READ:

Leviticus 20;
Mark 5;
Psalms 42–43

*Why art thou cast down, O my soul? and why art thou
disquieted within me? hope in God: for I shall yet praise
him, who is the health of my countenance, and my God.*
Psalm 43:5

DAY 59

Today's Date: _____

MY PRAYER FOR TODAY: ....
....
....

MY TAKEAWAY FROM TODAY'S BIBLE READING:
....
....
....

READ:

Leviticus 21–22;
Mark 6:1–13;
Psalm 44

*I am the LORD which hallow you, that brought you out
of the land of Egypt, to be your God: I am the LORD.*
LEVITICUS 22:32–33

DAY 60

Today's Date: _____

MY PRAYER FOR TODAY: ....
....
....

READ:

Leviticus 23–24;
Mark 6:14–29;
Psalm 45:1–5

MY TAKEAWAY FROM TODAY'S BIBLE READING:
....
....
....

*Six days shall work be done: but the seventh day is the sabbath
of rest, an holy convocation; ye shall do no work therein:
it is the sabbath of the LORD in all your dwellings.*
LEVITICUS 23:3

DAY 61

Today's Date: _____

📍 MY PRAYER FOR TODAY: ....
....
....

READ:

Leviticus 25;
Mark 6:30–56;
Psalm 45:6–12

MY TAKEAWAY FROM TODAY'S BIBLE READING:
....
....
....

Thy throne, O God, is for ever and ever:
the sceptre of thy kingdom is a right sceptre.
Psalm 45:6

DAY 62

Today's Date: _____

📍 MY PRAYER FOR TODAY: ....
....
....

MY TAKEAWAY FROM TODAY'S BIBLE READING:

READ:

Leviticus 26;
Mark 7;
Psalm 45:13–17

....
....
....

If ye walk in my statutes, and keep my commandments, and do them;
then I will give you rain in due season, and the land shall yield her
increase, and the trees of the field shall yield their fruit.
Leviticus 26:3–4

Today's Date: _____

MY PRAYER FOR TODAY: ....
....
....

MY TAKEAWAY FROM TODAY'S BIBLE READING:

....
....
....

READ:

Leviticus 27;
Mark 8;
Psalm 46

*Be still, and know that I am God: I will be exalted among
the heathen, I will be exalted in the earth. The LORD of
hosts is with us; the God of Jacob is our refuge. Selah.*
PSALM 46:10–11

Today's Date: _____

MY PRAYER FOR TODAY: ....
....
....

READ:

Numbers 1–2;
Mark 9:1–13;
Psalm 47

MY TAKEAWAY FROM TODAY'S BIBLE READING:

....
....
....

*O clap your hands, all ye people;
shout unto God with the voice of triumph.*
PSALM 47:1

DAY 65

Today's Date: _____

📍 MY PRAYER FOR TODAY: ....
....
....

READ:

Numbers 3;
Mark 9:14–50;
Psalm 48:1–8

MY TAKEAWAY FROM TODAY'S BIBLE READING:
....
....
....

*Jesus said unto him, If thou canst believe,
all things are possible to him that believeth.*
MARK 9:23

DAY 66

Today's Date: _____

📍 MY PRAYER FOR TODAY: ....
....
....

MY TAKEAWAY FROM TODAY'S BIBLE READING:
....
....
....

READ:

Numbers 4;
Mark 10:1–34;
Psalm 48:9–14

*For this God is our God for ever and ever:
he will be our guide even unto death.*
PSALM 48:14

Today's Date: _____

MY PRAYER FOR TODAY: ....
....
....

MY TAKEAWAY FROM TODAY'S BIBLE READING:
....
....
....

READ:

Numbers 5:1–6:21;
Mark 10:35–52;
Psalm 49:1–9

And whosoever of you will be the chiefest, shall be servant of all. For even the Son of man came not to be ministered unto, but to minister, and to give his life a ransom for many.
Mark 10:44–45

Today's Date: _____

MY PRAYER FOR TODAY: ....
....
....

READ:

Numbers 6:22–7:47;
Mark 11;
Psalm 49:10–20

MY TAKEAWAY FROM TODAY'S BIBLE READING:
....
....
....

God will redeem my soul from the power of the grave: for he shall receive me.
Psalm 49:15

DAY 69

Today's Date: _____

📍 MY PRAYER FOR TODAY: ....

....

....

READ:

Numbers 7:48–8:4;
Mark 12:1–27;
Psalm 50:1–15

MY TAKEAWAY FROM TODAY'S BIBLE READING:

....

....

....

*The mighty God, even the LORD, hath spoken, and called the
earth from the rising of the sun unto the going down thereof.*
PSALM 50:1

DAY 70

Today's Date: _____

📍 MY PRAYER FOR TODAY: ....

....

....

MY TAKEAWAY FROM TODAY'S BIBLE READING:

READ:

Numbers 8:5–9:23;
Mark 12:28–44;
Psalm 50:16–23

....

....

....

*Thou shalt love the Lord thy God with all thy heart,
and with all thy soul, and with all thy mind, and with all
thy strength. . . . Thou shalt love thy neighbour as thyself.*
MARK 12:30–31

DAY 71

Today's Date: _____

📍 MY PRAYER FOR TODAY: ....
....
....

MY TAKEAWAY FROM TODAY'S BIBLE READING:
....
....
....

READ:

NUMBERS 10–11;
MARK 13:1–8;
PSALM 51:1–9

*Have mercy upon me, O God, according to thy
lovingkindness: according unto the multitude
of thy tender mercies blot out my transgressions.*
PSALM 51:1

DAY 72

Today's Date: _____

📍 MY PRAYER FOR TODAY: ....
....
....

READ:

NUMBERS 12–13;
MARK 13:9–37;
PSALM 51:10–19

MY TAKEAWAY FROM TODAY'S BIBLE READING:
....
....
....

*Create in me a clean heart, O God;
and renew a right spirit within me.*
PSALM 51:10

DAY 73

Today's Date: _____

📍 MY PRAYER FOR TODAY: ....

....

....

READ:

Numbers 14;
Mark 14:1–31;
Psalm 52

MY TAKEAWAY FROM TODAY'S BIBLE READING:

....

....

....

*If the LORD delight in us, then he will bring us into this land,
and give it us; a land which floweth with milk and honey.*
NUMBERS 14:8

DAY 74

Today's Date: _____

📍 MY PRAYER FOR TODAY: ....

....

....

MY TAKEAWAY FROM TODAY'S BIBLE READING:

....

....

....

READ:

Numbers 15;
Mark 14:32–72;
Psalm 53

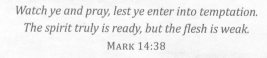

*Watch ye and pray, lest ye enter into temptation.
The spirit truly is ready, but the flesh is weak.*
MARK 14:38

Today's Date: _____

DAY 75

MY PRAYER FOR TODAY: ....
....
....

MY TAKEAWAY FROM TODAY'S BIBLE READING:
....
....
....

READ:

Numbers 16;
Mark 15:1–32;
Psalm 54

Hear my prayer, O God;
give ear to the words of my mouth.
Psalm 54:2

Today's Date: _____

DAY 76

MY PRAYER FOR TODAY: ....
....
....

READ:

Numbers 17–18;
Mark 15:33–47;
Psalm 55

MY TAKEAWAY FROM TODAY'S BIBLE READING:
....
....
....

Cast thy burden upon the Lord, and he shall sustain thee:
he shall never suffer the righteous to be moved.
Psalm 55:22

DAY 77

Today's Date: _____

📍 MY PRAYER FOR TODAY: ....
....
....

READ:

Numbers 19–20;
Mark 16;
Psalm 56:1–7

MY TAKEAWAY FROM TODAY'S BIBLE READING:
....
....
....

*In God I will praise his word, in God I have put
my trust; I will not fear what flesh can do unto me.*
PSALM 56:4

DAY 78

Today's Date: _____

📍 MY PRAYER FOR TODAY: ....
....
....

MY TAKEAWAY FROM TODAY'S BIBLE READING:
....
....
....

READ:

Numbers 21:1–22:20;
Luke 1:1–25;
Psalm 56:8–13

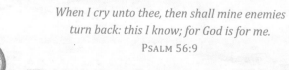

*When I cry unto thee, then shall mine enemies
turn back: this I know; for God is for me.*
PSALM 56:9

DAY 79

Today's Date: _____

MY PRAYER FOR TODAY: ....
....
....

MY TAKEAWAY FROM TODAY'S BIBLE READING:
....
....
....

READ:

Numbers 22:21–23:30;
Luke 1:26–56;
Psalm 57

*Be merciful unto me, O God, be merciful unto me: for my
soul trusteth in thee: yea, in the shadow of thy wings will
I make my refuge, until these calamities be overpast.*
Psalm 57:1

DAY 80

Today's Date: _____

MY PRAYER FOR TODAY: ....
....
....

READ:

Numbers 24–25;
Luke 1:57–2:20;
Psalm 58

MY TAKEAWAY FROM TODAY'S BIBLE READING:
....
....
....

*Fear not: for, behold, I bring you good tidings of great joy,
which shall be to all people. For unto you is born this day
in the city of David a Saviour, which is Christ the Lord.*
Luke 2:10–11

DAY 81 Today's Date: _____

📍 MY PRAYER FOR TODAY: ....
....
....

READ:

Numbers 26:1–27:11;
Luke 2:21–38;
Psalm 59:1–8

MY TAKEAWAY FROM TODAY'S BIBLE READING:

....
....
....

*Lord. . .mine eyes have seen thy salvation, which thou
hast prepared before the face of all people; a light to
lighten the Gentiles, and the glory of thy people Israel.*
LUKE 2:29–32

DAY 82 Today's Date: _____

📍 MY PRAYER FOR TODAY: ....
....
....

MY TAKEAWAY FROM TODAY'S BIBLE READING:

....
....
....

READ:

Numbers 27:12–
29:11;
Luke 2:39–52;
Psalm 59:9–17

*But I will sing of thy power; yea, I will sing aloud of
thy mercy in the morning: for thou hast been my
defence and refuge in the day of my trouble.*
PSALM 59:16

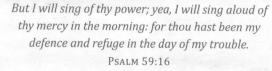

Today's Date: _____

📍 MY PRAYER FOR TODAY: ....
....
....

MY TAKEAWAY FROM TODAY'S BIBLE READING:

READ:
NUMBERS 29:12–
30:16;
LUKE 3;
PSALM 60:1–5

....
....
....

All flesh shall see the salvation of God.
LUKE 3:6

Today's Date: _____

📍 MY PRAYER FOR TODAY: ....
....
....

READ:

NUMBERS 31;
LUKE 4;
PSALM 60:6–12

MY TAKEAWAY FROM TODAY'S BIBLE READING:

....
....
....

Give us help from trouble: for vain is the help of man.
Through God we shall do valiantly: for he it is
that shall tread down our enemies.
PSALM 60:11–12

DAY 85   Today's Date: _____

⦿ MY PRAYER FOR TODAY: ....
....
....

READ:

Numbers 32–33;
Luke 5:1–16;
Psalm 61

MY TAKEAWAY FROM TODAY'S BIBLE READING:
....
....
....

*Hear my cry, O God; attend unto my prayer. From the
end of the earth will I cry unto thee, when my heart is
overwhelmed: lead me to the rock that is higher than I.*
Psalm 61:1–2

DAY 86   Today's Date: _____

⦿ MY PRAYER FOR TODAY: ....
....
....

MY TAKEAWAY FROM TODAY'S BIBLE READING:
....
....
....

READ:

Numbers 34–36;
Luke 5:17–32;
Psalm 62:1–6

*He only is my rock and my salvation:
he is my defence; I shall not be moved.*
Psalm 62:6

Today's Date: _____

MY PRAYER FOR TODAY: ....

....

....

MY TAKEAWAY FROM TODAY'S BIBLE READING:

....

....

....

READ:

DEUTERONOMY
1:1–2:25;
LUKE 5:33–6:11;
PSALM 62:7–12

*In God is my salvation and my glory: the rock
of my strength, and my refuge, is in God.*
PSALM 62:7

Today's Date: _____

DAY 88

MY PRAYER FOR TODAY: ....

....

....

READ:

DEUTERONOMY
2:26–4:14;
LUKE 6:12–35;
PSALM 63:1–5

MY TAKEAWAY FROM TODAY'S BIBLE READING:

....

....

....

*And [Jesus] lifted up his eyes on his disciples, and said,
Blessed be ye poor: for yours is the kingdom of God.*
LUKE 6:20

DAY 89

Today's Date: _____

📍 MY PRAYER FOR TODAY: ....
....
....

READ:

DEUTERONOMY
4:15–5:22;
LUKE 6:36–49;
PSALM 63:6–11

MY TAKEAWAY FROM TODAY'S BIBLE READING:
....
....
....

But if from thence thou shalt seek the LORD thy God, thou shalt find him, if thou seek him with all thy heart and with all thy soul.
DEUTERONOMY 4:29

DAY 90

Today's Date: _____

📍 MY PRAYER FOR TODAY: ....
....
....

MY TAKEAWAY FROM TODAY'S BIBLE READING:
....
....

READ:

DEUTERONOMY
5:23–7:26;
LUKE 7:1–17;
PSALM 64:1–5

Hear my voice, O God, in my prayer: preserve my life from fear of the enemy.
PSALM 64:1

Today's Date: _____

MY PRAYER FOR TODAY: ....
....
....

MY TAKEAWAY FROM TODAY'S BIBLE READING:
....
....
....

READ:

DEUTERONOMY 8–9;
LUKE 7:18–35;
PSALM 64:6–10

*The righteous shall be glad in the LORD, and shall trust
in him; and all the upright in heart shall glory.*
PSALM 64:10

Today's Date: _____

DAY 92

MY PRAYER FOR TODAY: ....
....
....

READ:

DEUTERONOMY 10–11;
LUKE 7:36–8:3;
PSALM 65:1–8

MY TAKEAWAY FROM TODAY'S BIBLE READING:
....
....
....

*O God of our salvation; who art the confidence of all the ends
of the earth, and of them that are afar off upon the sea. . .*
PSALM 65:5

DAY 93

Today's Date: _____

📍 MY PRAYER FOR TODAY: ....
....
....

READ:

Deuteronomy 12–13;
Luke 8:4–21;
Psalm 65:9–13

MY TAKEAWAY FROM TODAY'S BIBLE READING:
....
....
....

The little hills rejoice on every side. The pastures are clothed with flocks; the valleys also are covered over with corn; they shout for joy, they also sing.
PSALM 65:12–13

DAY 94

Today's Date: _____

📍 MY PRAYER FOR TODAY: ....
....
....

MY TAKEAWAY FROM TODAY'S BIBLE READING:
....
....

READ:

Deuteronomy
14:1–16:8;
Luke 8:22–39;
Psalm 66:1–7

And he said. . .Where is your faith? And they being afraid wondered, saying one to another, What manner of man is this! for he commandeth even the winds and water, and they obey him.
LUKE 8:25

Today's Date: _____

📍 MY PRAYER FOR TODAY: ....
....
....

MY TAKEAWAY FROM TODAY'S BIBLE READING:

READ:
Deuteronomy
16:9–18:22;
Luke 8:40–56;
Psalm 66:8–15

....
....
....

*O bless our God, ye people, and make
the voice of his praise to be heard.*
PSALM 66:8

Today's Date: _____

DAY 96

📍 MY PRAYER FOR TODAY: ....
....
....

READ:
Deuteronomy
19:1–21:9;
Luke 9:1–22;
Psalm 66:16–20

MY TAKEAWAY FROM TODAY'S BIBLE READING:

....
....
....

*Hear, O Israel, ye approach this day unto battle against your enemies:
let not your hearts faint, fear not, and do not tremble. . .for the LORD
your God is he that goeth with you. . .to save you.*
DEUTERONOMY 20:3–4

DAY 97

Today's Date: _____

📍 MY PRAYER FOR TODAY: ....
....
....

READ:

Deuteronomy
21:10–23:8;
Luke 9:23–42;
Psalm 67

MY TAKEAWAY FROM TODAY'S BIBLE READING:
....
....
....

*God be merciful unto us, and bless us; and cause his face
to shine upon us; Selah. That thy way may be known
upon earth, thy saving health among all nations.*
Psalm 67:1–2

DAY 98

Today's Date: _____

📍 MY PRAYER FOR TODAY: ....
....
....

MY TAKEAWAY FROM TODAY'S BIBLE READING:
....
....
....

READ:

Deuteronomy
23:9–25:19;
Luke 9:43–62;
Psalm 68:1–6

*A father of the fatherless, and a judge of the widows, is God
in his holy habitation. God setteth the solitary in families.*
Psalm 68:5–6

Today's Date: _____

DAY 99

MY PRAYER FOR TODAY: ....
....
....

MY TAKEAWAY FROM TODAY'S BIBLE READING:

....
....
....

READ:
DEUTERONOMY
26:1–28:14;
LUKE 10:1–20;
PSALM 68:7–14

Notwithstanding in this rejoice not, that the spirits are subject unto you; but rather rejoice, because your names are written in heaven.
LUKE 10:20

Today's Date: _____

DAY 100

MY PRAYER FOR TODAY: ....
....
....

READ:
DEUTERONOMY
28:15–68;
LUKE 10:21–37;
PSALM 68:15–19

MY TAKEAWAY FROM TODAY'S BIBLE READING:

....
....
....

Blessed be the Lord, who daily loadeth us with benefits, even the God of our salvation. Selah.
PSALM 68:19

DAY 101 Today's Date: _____

📍 MY PRAYER FOR TODAY: ....
....
....

READ:

Deuteronomy 29–30;
Luke 10:38–11:23;
Psalm 68:20–27

MY TAKEAWAY FROM TODAY'S BIBLE READING:
....
....
....

*I call heaven and earth to record this day against you,
that I have set before you life and death, blessing and cursing:
therefore choose life, that both thou and thy seed may live.*
Deuteronomy 30:19

DAY 102 Today's Date: _____

📍 MY PRAYER FOR TODAY: ....
....
....

MY TAKEAWAY FROM TODAY'S BIBLE READING:
....
....
....

READ:

Deuteronomy
31:1–32:22;
Luke 11:24–36;
Psalm 68:28–35

*Be strong and of a good courage, fear not, nor be afraid
of them: for the Lord thy God, he it is that doth go
with thee; he will not fail thee, nor forsake thee.*
Deuteronomy 31:6

Today's Date: _____ **DAY 103**

MY PRAYER FOR TODAY: ....
....
....

MY TAKEAWAY FROM TODAY'S BIBLE READING:

....

....

....

READ:

DEUTERONOMY
32:23–33:29;
LUKE 11:37–54;
PSALM 69:1–9

Save me, O God; for the waters are come in unto my soul.
PSALM 69:1

Today's Date: _____ **DAY 104**

MY PRAYER FOR TODAY: ....
....
....

READ:

DEUTERONOMY 34–
JOSHUA 2;
LUKE 12:1–15;
PSALM 69:10–17

MY TAKEAWAY FROM TODAY'S BIBLE READING:

....

....

....

*Hear me, O LORD; for thy lovingkindness is good: turn unto
me according to the multitude of thy tender mercies.*
PSALM 69:16

DAY 105   Today's Date: _____

📍 MY PRAYER FOR TODAY: ....

....

....

READ:

Joshua 3:1–5:12;
Luke 12:16–40;
Psalm 69:18–28

MY TAKEAWAY FROM TODAY'S BIBLE READING:

....

....

....

*Consider the ravens: for they neither sow nor reap;
which neither have storehouse nor barn; and God feedeth
them: how much more are ye better than the fowls?*
Luke 12:24

DAY 106   Today's Date: _____

📍 MY PRAYER FOR TODAY: ....

....

....

MY TAKEAWAY FROM TODAY'S BIBLE READING:

READ:

Joshua 5:13–7:26;
Luke 12:41–48;
Psalm 69:29–36

....

....

....

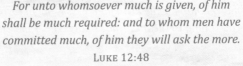

*For unto whomsoever much is given, of him
shall be much required: and to whom men have
committed much, of him they will ask the more.*
Luke 12:48

Today's Date: _____

⊙ MY PRAYER FOR TODAY: ....
....
....

MY TAKEAWAY FROM TODAY'S BIBLE READING:
....
....
....

READ:

Joshua 8–9;
Luke 12:49–59;
Psalm 70

*I am poor and needy: make haste unto me, O God: thou art
my help and my deliverer; O Lord, make no tarrying.*
Psalm 70:5

Today's Date: _____

⊙ MY PRAYER FOR TODAY: ....
....
....

READ:

Joshua 10:1–11:15;
Luke 13:1–21;
Psalm 71:1–6

MY TAKEAWAY FROM TODAY'S BIBLE READING:
....
....
....

*For thou art my hope, O Lord God:
thou art my trust from my youth.*
Psalm 71:5

DAY 109   Today's Date: _____

MY PRAYER FOR TODAY: ....
....
....

READ:

Joshua 11:16–13:33;
Luke 13:22–35;
Psalm 71:7–16

MY TAKEAWAY FROM TODAY'S BIBLE READING:
....
....
....

*But I will hope continually, and will
yet praise thee more and more.*
Psalm 71:14

DAY 110   Today's Date: _____

MY PRAYER FOR TODAY: ....
....
....

MY TAKEAWAY FROM TODAY'S BIBLE READING:
....
....
....

READ:

Joshua 14–16;
Luke 14:1–15;
Psalm 71:17–21

*Thou shalt increase my greatness,
and comfort me on every side.*
Psalm 71:21

Today's Date: _____

MY PRAYER FOR TODAY: ....

....

....

MY TAKEAWAY FROM TODAY'S BIBLE READING:

....

....

....

READ:

Joshua 17:1–19:16;
Luke 14:16–35;
Psalm 71:22–24

*So likewise, whosoever he be of you that forsaketh
not all that he hath, he cannot be my disciple.*
LUKE 14:33

Today's Date: _____

MY PRAYER FOR TODAY: ....

....

....

READ:

Joshua 19:17–21:42;
Luke 15:1–10;
Psalm 72:1–11

MY TAKEAWAY FROM TODAY'S BIBLE READING:

....

....

....

*Likewise, I say unto you, there is joy in the presence
of the angels of God over one sinner that repenteth.*
LUKE 15:10

DAY 113

Today's Date: _____

⚲ MY PRAYER FOR TODAY: ....
....
....

READ:

Joshua 21:43–22:34;
Luke 15:11–32;
Psalm 72:12–20

MY TAKEAWAY FROM TODAY'S BIBLE READING:
....
....
....

*There failed not ought of any good thing which the Lord
had spoken unto the house of Israel; all came to pass.*
Joshua 21:45

DAY 114

Today's Date: _____

⚲ MY PRAYER FOR TODAY: ....
....
....

MY TAKEAWAY FROM TODAY'S BIBLE READING:
....
....
....

READ:

Joshua 23–24;
Luke 16:1–18;
Psalm 73:1–9

*No servant can serve two masters: for either he will hate
the one, and love the other; or else he will hold to the one,
and despise the other. Ye cannot serve God and mammon.*
Luke 16:13

Today's Date: _____   **DAY 115**

📍 MY PRAYER FOR TODAY: ....
....
....

MY TAKEAWAY FROM TODAY'S BIBLE READING:
....

....

....

READ:

Judges 1–2;
Luke 16:19–17:10;
Psalm 73:10–20

If ye had faith as a grain of mustard seed, ye might say unto this sycamine tree, Be thou plucked up by the root, and be thou planted in the sea; and it should obey you.
Luke 17:6

Today's Date: _____   **DAY 116**

📍 MY PRAYER FOR TODAY: ....
....

READ:

Judges 3–4;
Luke 17:11–37;
Psalm 73:21–28

MY TAKEAWAY FROM TODAY'S BIBLE READING:
....

....

....

My flesh and my heart faileth: but God is the strength of my heart, and my portion for ever.
Psalm 73:26

DAY 117   Today's Date: _____

⊙ MY PRAYER FOR TODAY: ....
....
....

READ:

Judges 5:1–6:24;
Luke 18:1–17;
Psalm 74:1–3

MY TAKEAWAY FROM TODAY'S BIBLE READING:

....
....
....

Suffer little children to come unto me, and forbid them not: for of such is the kingdom of God. . . . Whosoever shall not receive the kingdom of God as a little child shall in no wise enter therein.
Luke 18:16–17

DAY 118   Today's Date: _____

⊙ MY PRAYER FOR TODAY: ....
....
....

MY TAKEAWAY FROM TODAY'S BIBLE READING:

READ:

Judges 6:25–7:25;
Luke 18:18–43;
Psalm 74:4–11

....
....
....

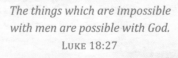

The things which are impossible with men are possible with God.
Luke 18:27

Today's Date: _____

📍 MY PRAYER FOR TODAY: ....
....
....
....

MY TAKEAWAY FROM TODAY'S BIBLE READING:
....
....
....

READ:

JUDGES 8:1–9:23;
LUKE 19:1–28;
PSALM 74:12–17

*For God is my King of old, working
salvation in the midst of the earth.*
PSALM 74:12

Today's Date: _____

📍 MY PRAYER FOR TODAY: ....
....
....

READ:

JUDGES 9:24–10:18;
LUKE 19:29–48;
PSALM 74:18–23

MY TAKEAWAY FROM TODAY'S BIBLE READING:
....
....
....

*O let not the oppressed return ashamed:
let the poor and needy praise thy name.*
PSALM 74:21

DAY 121 Today's Date: _____

📍 MY PRAYER FOR TODAY: ....
....
....

READ:

Judges 11:1–12:7;
Luke 20:1–26;
Psalm 75:1–7

MY TAKEAWAY FROM TODAY'S BIBLE READING:
....
....
....

*For promotion cometh neither from the east, nor from
the west, nor from the south. But God is the judge:
he putteth down one, and setteth up another.*
PSALM 75:6–7

DAY 122 Today's Date: _____

📍 MY PRAYER FOR TODAY: ....
....
....

MY TAKEAWAY FROM TODAY'S BIBLE READING:
....

READ:

Judges 12:8–14:20;
Luke 20:27–47;
Psalm 75:8–10

....
....

*I will declare for ever; I will sing
praises to the God of Jacob.*
PSALM 75:9

Today's Date: _____

📍 MY PRAYER FOR TODAY: ....
....
....

MY TAKEAWAY FROM TODAY'S BIBLE READING:
....
....
....

READ:

Judges 15–16;
Luke 21:1–19;
Psalm 76:1–7

*This poor widow hath cast in more than they all: for all these
have of their abundance cast in unto the offerings of God:
but she of her penury hath cast in all the living that she had.*
Luke 21:3–4

Today's Date: _____

📍 MY PRAYER FOR TODAY: ....
....
....

READ:

Judges 17–18;
Luke 21:20–22:6;
Psalm 76:8–12

MY TAKEAWAY FROM TODAY'S BIBLE READING:
....
....

*Heaven and earth shall pass away:
but my words shall not pass away.*
Luke 21:33

DAY 125 Today's Date: _____

⊙ MY PRAYER FOR TODAY: ....
....
....

READ:

Judges 19:1–20:23;
Luke 22:7–30;
Psalm 77:1–11

MY TAKEAWAY FROM TODAY'S BIBLE READING:
....
....
....

*Hath God forgotten to be gracious? hath he in anger shut
up his tender mercies? Selah. . . . I will remember the works
of the Lord: surely I will remember thy wonders of old.*
Psalm 77:9, 11

DAY 126 Today's Date: _____

⊙ MY PRAYER FOR TODAY: ....
....
....

MY TAKEAWAY FROM TODAY'S BIBLE READING:
....
....
....

READ:

Judges 20:24–21:25;
Luke 22:31–54;
Psalm 77:12–20

*Thou art the God that doest wonders:
thou hast declared thy strength among the people.*
Psalm 77:14

Today's Date: _____

MY PRAYER FOR TODAY: ....
....
....

MY TAKEAWAY FROM TODAY'S BIBLE READING:
....
....
....

READ:

Ruth 1–2;
Luke 22:55–23:25;
Psalm 78:1–4

Give ear, O my people, to my law:
incline your ears to the words of my mouth.
Psalm 78:1

Today's Date: _____

MY PRAYER FOR TODAY: ....
....
....

READ:

Ruth 3–4;
Luke 23:26–24:12;
Psalm 78:5–8

MY TAKEAWAY FROM TODAY'S BIBLE READING:
....
....
....

That the generation to come might know them, even the children
which should be born. . .that they might set their hope in God,
and not forget the works of God, but keep his commandments.
Psalm 78:6–7

DAY 129 Today's Date: _____

📍 MY PRAYER FOR TODAY: ....
....
....

READ:

1 Samuel 1:1–2:21;
Luke 24:13–53;
Psalm 78:9–16

MY TAKEAWAY FROM TODAY'S BIBLE READING:
....
....
....

The Lord is risen indeed.
Luke 24:34

DAY 130 Today's Date: _____

📍 MY PRAYER FOR TODAY: ....
....
....

MY TAKEAWAY FROM TODAY'S BIBLE READING:
....
....
....

READ:

1 Samuel 2:22–4:22;
John 1:1–28;
Psalm 78:17–24

*In the beginning was the Word, and the Word was with God,
and the Word was God. . . . And the Word was made flesh,
and dwelt among us. . .full of grace and truth.*
John 1:1, 14

Today's Date: _____   **DAY 131**

📍 MY PRAYER FOR TODAY: ....
....
....

MY TAKEAWAY FROM TODAY'S BIBLE READING:

....

....

....

READ:

1 Samuel 5–7;
John 1:29–51;
Psalm 78:25–33

> *Behold the Lamb of God, which taketh*
> *away the sin of the world.*
> John 1:29

Today's Date: _____   **DAY 132**

📍 MY PRAYER FOR TODAY: ....
....
....

READ:

1 Samuel 8:1–9:26;
John 2;
Psalm 78:34–41

MY TAKEAWAY FROM TODAY'S BIBLE READING:

....

....

....

> *[God,] being full of compassion, forgave their iniquity,*
> *and destroyed them not: yea, many a time turned he*
> *his anger away, and did not stir up all his wrath.*
> Psalm 78:38

DAY 133   Today's Date: _____

📍 MY PRAYER FOR TODAY: ....
....
....

READ:

1 Samuel 9:27–11:15;
John 3:1–22;
Psalm 78:42–55

MY TAKEAWAY FROM TODAY'S BIBLE READING:

....
....
....

Marvel not that I said unto thee,
Ye must be born again.
John 3:7

DAY 134   Today's Date: _____

📍 MY PRAYER FOR TODAY: ....
....
....

MY TAKEAWAY FROM TODAY'S BIBLE READING:

....
....
....

READ:

1 Samuel 12–13;
John 3:23–4:10;
Psalm 78:56–66

He that believeth on the Son hath everlasting life:
and he that believeth not the Son shall not see life;
but the wrath of God abideth on him.
John 3:36

Today's Date: _____ **DAY 135**

📍 MY PRAYER FOR TODAY: ....
....
....

MY TAKEAWAY FROM TODAY'S BIBLE READING:

READ:

1 Samuel 14;
John 4:11–38;
Psalm 78:67–72

....
....
....

*Whosoever drinketh of the water that I shall give him shall
never thirst; but the water that I shall give him shall be in
him a well of water springing up into everlasting life.*
John 4:14

Today's Date: _____ **DAY 136**

📍 MY PRAYER FOR TODAY: ....
....
....

READ:

1 Samuel 15–16;
John 4:39–54;
Psalm 79:1–7

MY TAKEAWAY FROM TODAY'S BIBLE READING:

....
....
....

*The Lord seeth not as man seeth; for man looketh on the
outward appearance, but the Lord looketh on the heart.*
1 Samuel 16:7

DAY 137 Today's Date: _____

MY PRAYER FOR TODAY: ....
....
....

READ:

1 Samuel 17;
John 5:1–24;
Psalm 79:8–13

MY TAKEAWAY FROM TODAY'S BIBLE READING:
....
....
....

Help us, O God of our salvation, for the glory of thy name:
and deliver us, and purge away our sins, for thy name's sake.
PSALM 79:9

DAY 138 Today's Date: _____

MY PRAYER FOR TODAY: ....
....
....

MY TAKEAWAY FROM TODAY'S BIBLE READING:
....
....
....

READ:

1 Samuel 18–19;
John 5:25–47;
Psalm 80:1–7

Turn us again, O God of hosts, and cause
thy face to shine; and we shall be saved.
PSALM 80:7

Today's Date: _____   **DAY 139**

📍 MY PRAYER FOR TODAY: ....
....
....

MY TAKEAWAY FROM TODAY'S BIBLE READING:

....
....
....

READ:

1 SAMUEL 20–21;
JOHN 6:1–21;
PSALM 80:8–19

[Jesus] saith unto them,
It is I; be not afraid.
JOHN 6:20

Today's Date: _____   **DAY 140**

📍 MY PRAYER FOR TODAY: ....
....
....

READ:

1 SAMUEL 22–23;
JOHN 6:22–42;
PSALM 81:1–10

MY TAKEAWAY FROM TODAY'S BIBLE READING:

....
....
....

I am the LORD thy God, which brought thee out of the
land of Egypt: open thy mouth wide, and I will fill it.
PSALM 81:10

DAY 141 — Today's Date: _____

📍 MY PRAYER FOR TODAY: ....
....
....

READ:

1 Samuel 24:1–25:31;
John 6:43–71;
Psalm 81:11–16

MY TAKEAWAY FROM TODAY'S BIBLE READING:
....
....
....

*Verily, verily, I say unto you, He that
believeth on me hath everlasting life.*
John 6:47

DAY 142 — Today's Date: _____

📍 MY PRAYER FOR TODAY: ....
....
....

MY TAKEAWAY FROM TODAY'S BIBLE READING:

READ:

1 Samuel 25:32–
27:12;
John 7:1–24;
Psalm 82

....
....
....

*Arise, O God, judge the earth:
for thou shalt inherit all nations.*
Psalm 82:8

Today's Date: _____

MY PRAYER FOR TODAY: ....
....
....

MY TAKEAWAY FROM TODAY'S BIBLE READING:
....
....
....
....

READ:

1 SAMUEL 28–29;
JOHN 7:25–8:11;
PSALM 83

*That men may know that thou, whose name alone
is JEHOVAH, art the most high over all the earth.*
PSALM 83:18

Today's Date: _____

MY PRAYER FOR TODAY: ....
....
....

READ:

1 SAMUEL 30–31;
JOHN 8:12–47;
PSALM 84:1–4

MY TAKEAWAY FROM TODAY'S BIBLE READING:
....
....
....

*My soul longeth, yea, even fainteth for the courts of the LORD:
my heart and my flesh crieth out for the living God.*
PSALM 84:2

DAY 145 Today's Date: _____

📍 MY PRAYER FOR TODAY: ....
....
....

READ:

2 Samuel 1–2;
John 8:48–9:12;
Psalm 84:5–12

MY TAKEAWAY FROM TODAY'S BIBLE READING:
....
....
....

For the Lord God is a sun and shield: the Lord will give grace and glory: no good thing will he withhold from them that walk uprightly.
Psalm 84:11

DAY 146 Today's Date: _____

📍 MY PRAYER FOR TODAY: ....
....
....

MY TAKEAWAY FROM TODAY'S BIBLE READING:

READ:

2 Samuel 3–4;
John 9:13–34;
Psalm 85:1–7

....
....
....

Shew us thy mercy, O Lord, and grant us thy salvation.
Psalm 85:7

Today's Date: _____

MY PRAYER FOR TODAY: ....
....
....

MY TAKEAWAY FROM TODAY'S BIBLE READING:
....
....
....

READ:

2 Samuel 5:1–7:17;
John 9:35–10:10;
Psalm 85:8–13

And David danced before
the Lord with all his might.
2 Samuel 6:14

Today's Date: _____

MY PRAYER FOR TODAY: ....
....
....

READ:

2 Samuel 7:18–10:19;
John 10:11–30;
Psalm 86:1–10

MY TAKEAWAY FROM TODAY'S BIBLE READING:
....
....
....

I am the good shepherd, and know my sheep, and am
known of mine. As the Father knoweth me, even so
know I the Father: and I lay down my life for the sheep.
John 10:14–15

DAY 149 — Today's Date: _____

📍 MY PRAYER FOR TODAY: ....
....
....

READ:

2 Samuel 11:1–12:25;
John 10:31–11:16;
Psalm 86:11–17

MY TAKEAWAY FROM TODAY'S BIBLE READING:
....
....
....

I will praise thee, O Lord my God, with all my heart:
and I will glorify thy name for evermore.
PSALM 86:12

DAY 150 — Today's Date: _____

📍 MY PRAYER FOR TODAY: ....
....
....

MY TAKEAWAY FROM TODAY'S BIBLE READING:
....
....
....

READ:

2 Samuel 12:26–
13:39;
John 11:17–54;
Psalm 87

Jesus said. . .I am the resurrection, and the life: he that believeth
in me, though he were dead, yet shall he live: and whosoever
liveth and believeth in me shall never die. Believest thou this?
JOHN 11:25–26

Today's Date: _____

MY PRAYER FOR TODAY: ....
....
....

MY TAKEAWAY FROM TODAY'S BIBLE READING:
....
....
....

READ:

2 SAMUEL 14:1–15:12;
JOHN 11:55–12:19;
PSALM 88:1–9

*O lord God of my salvation, I have cried day and night before thee:
let my prayer come before thee: incline thine ear unto my cry.*
PSALM 88:1–2

Today's Date: _____

MY PRAYER FOR TODAY: ....
....
....

READ:

2 SAMUEL 15:13–
16:23;
JOHN 12:20–43;
PSALM 88:10–18

MY TAKEAWAY FROM TODAY'S BIBLE READING:
....
....
....

*He that loveth his life shall lose it; and he that hateth
his life in this world shall keep it unto life eternal.*
JOHN 12:25

DAY 153   Today's Date: _____

📍 MY PRAYER FOR TODAY: ....
....
....

READ:

2 Samuel 17:1–18:18;
John 12:44–13:20;
Psalm 89:1–6

MY TAKEAWAY FROM TODAY'S BIBLE READING:
....
....
....

If I then, your Lord and Master, have washed your feet;
ye also ought to wash one another's feet. For I have given
you an example, that ye should do as I have done to you.
John 13:14–15

DAY 154   Today's Date: _____

📍 MY PRAYER FOR TODAY: ....
....
....

MY TAKEAWAY FROM TODAY'S BIBLE READING:

READ:

2 Samuel 18:19–
19:39;
John 13:21–38;
Psalm 89:7–13

....
....
....

Thou rulest the raging of the sea: when the
waves thereof arise, thou stillest them.
Psalm 89:9

Today's Date: _____

DAY 155

MY PRAYER FOR TODAY: ....
....
....

MY TAKEAWAY FROM TODAY'S BIBLE READING:
....
....
....

READ:
2 Samuel 19:40–
21:22;
John 14:1–17;
Psalm 89:14–18

And I will pray the Father, and he shall give you another
Comforter, that he may abide with you for ever.
John 14:16

Today's Date: _____

DAY 156

MY PRAYER FOR TODAY: ....
....
....

READ:
2 Samuel 22:1–23:7;
John 14:18–15:27;
Psalm 89:19–29

MY TAKEAWAY FROM TODAY'S BIBLE READING:
....
....
....

For thou art my lamp, O Lord: and the
Lord will lighten my darkness.
2 Samuel 22:29

DAY 157

Today's Date: _____

📍 MY PRAYER FOR TODAY: ....
....
....

READ:

2 Samuel 23:8–24:25;
John 16:1–22;
Psalm 89:30–37

MY TAKEAWAY FROM TODAY'S BIBLE READING:
....
....
....

Nevertheless my lovingkindness will I not utterly take from him, nor suffer my faithfulness to fail. My covenant will I not break, nor alter the thing that is gone out of my lips.
PSALM 89:33–34

DAY 158

Today's Date: _____

📍 MY PRAYER FOR TODAY: ....
....
....

MY TAKEAWAY FROM TODAY'S BIBLE READING:

READ:

1 Kings 1;
John 16:23–17:5;
Psalm 89:38–52

....
....
....

These things I have spoken unto you, that in me ye might have peace. In the world ye shall have tribulation: but be of good cheer; I have overcome the world.
JOHN 16:33

DAY 159

Today's Date: _____

📍 MY PRAYER FOR TODAY: ....
....
....

MY TAKEAWAY FROM TODAY'S BIBLE READING:
....
....
....

READ:

1 Kings 2;
John 17:6–26;
Psalm 90:1–12

*Before the mountains were brought forth,
or ever thou hadst formed the earth and the world,
even from everlasting to everlasting, thou art God.*
Psalm 90:2

DAY 160

Today's Date: _____

📍 MY PRAYER FOR TODAY: ....
....
....

READ:

1 Kings 3–4;
John 18:1–27;
Psalm 90:13–17

MY TAKEAWAY FROM TODAY'S BIBLE READING:
....
....
....

*Give therefore thy servant an understanding heart to judge
thy people, that I may discern between good and bad:
for who is able to judge this thy so great a people?*
1 Kings 3:9

DAY 161 Today's Date: _____

MY PRAYER FOR TODAY: ....
....
....

READ:

1 Kings 5–6;
John 18:28–19:5;
Psalm 91:1–10

MY TAKEAWAY FROM TODAY'S BIBLE READING:
....
....
....

*I will say of the Lord, He is my refuge and
my fortress: my God; in him will I trust.*
Psalm 91:2

DAY 162 Today's Date: _____

MY PRAYER FOR TODAY: ....
....
....

MY TAKEAWAY FROM TODAY'S BIBLE READING:
....
....

READ:

1 Kings 7;
John 19:6–24;
Psalm 91:11–16

*Because he hath set his love upon me, therefore will I deliver him:
I will set him on high, because he hath known my name.*
Psalm 91:14

Today's Date: _____ **DAY 163**

MY PRAYER FOR TODAY: ....

....

....

MY TAKEAWAY FROM TODAY'S BIBLE READING:

....

....

....

READ:

1 Kings 8:1–53;
John 19:25–42;
Psalm 92:1–9

*It is a good thing to give thanks unto the Lord, and to
sing praises unto thy name, O Most High: to shew forth thy
lovingkindness in the morning, and thy faithfulness every night.*
Psalm 92:1–2

Today's Date: _____ **DAY 164**

MY PRAYER FOR TODAY: ....

....

....

READ:

1 Kings 8:54–10:13;
John 20:1–18;
Psalm 92:10–15

MY TAKEAWAY FROM TODAY'S BIBLE READING:

....

....

....

*Those that be planted in the house of the
Lord shall flourish in the courts of our God.*
Psalm 92:13

DAY 165 Today's Date:

📍 MY PRAYER FOR TODAY: ....
....
....

READ:

1 Kings 10:14–11:43;
John 20:19–31;
Psalm 93

MY TAKEAWAY FROM TODAY'S BIBLE READING:
....
....
....

*But these are written, that ye might believe that Jesus is the Christ, the
Son of God; and that believing ye might have life through his name.*
JOHN 20:31

DAY 166 Today's Date: _____

📍 MY PRAYER FOR TODAY: ....
....
....

MY TAKEAWAY FROM TODAY'S BIBLE READING:
....
....
....

READ:

1 Kings 12:1–13:10;
John 21;
Psalm 94:1–11

Feed my sheep.
JOHN 21:17

Today's Date: _____

DAY 167

MY PRAYER FOR TODAY: ....
....
....

MY TAKEAWAY FROM TODAY'S BIBLE READING:
....
....
....

READ:

1 Kings 13:11–14:31;
Acts 1:1–11;
Psalm 94:12–23

Blessed is the man whom thou chastenest,
O Lord, and teachest him out of thy law.
Psalm 94:12

Today's Date: _____

DAY 168

MY PRAYER FOR TODAY: ....
....
....

READ:

1 Kings 15:1–16:20;
Acts 1:12–26;
Psalm 95

MY TAKEAWAY FROM TODAY'S BIBLE READING:
....
....
....

O come, let us sing unto the Lord: let us
make a joyful noise to the rock of our salvation.
Psalm 95:1

DAY 169   Today's Date: _____

MY PRAYER FOR TODAY: ....
....
....

READ:

1 Kings 16:21–18:19;
Acts 2:1–21;
Psalm 96:1–8

MY TAKEAWAY FROM TODAY'S BIBLE READING:
....
....
....

O sing unto the LORD a new song:
sing unto the LORD, all the earth.
PSALM 96:1

DAY 170   Today's Date: _____

MY PRAYER FOR TODAY: ....
....
....

MY TAKEAWAY FROM TODAY'S BIBLE READING:
....
....
....

READ:

1 Kings 18:20–19:21;
Acts 2:22–41;
Psalm 96:9–13

Thou hast made known to me the ways of life;
thou shalt make me full of joy with thy countenance.
ACTS 2:28

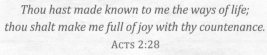

Today's Date: _____

MY PRAYER FOR TODAY: ....
....
....

MY TAKEAWAY FROM TODAY'S BIBLE READING:

....

....

....

READ:

1 KINGS 20;
ACTS 2:42–3:26;
PSALM 97:1–6

The LORD reigneth; let the earth rejoice;
let the multitude of isles be glad thereof.
PSALM 97:1

Today's Date: _____

MY PRAYER FOR TODAY: ....
....
....

READ:

1 KINGS 21:1–22:28;
ACTS 4:1–22;
PSALM 97:7–12

MY TAKEAWAY FROM TODAY'S BIBLE READING:

....

....

....

Ye that love the LORD, hate evil: he preserveth the souls of
his saints; he delivereth them out of the hand of the wicked.
PSALM 97:10

DAY 173   Today's Date: _____

⚲ MY PRAYER FOR TODAY: ....
....
....

READ:

1 Kings 22:29–
2 Kings 1;
Acts 4:23–5:11;
Psalm 98

MY TAKEAWAY FROM TODAY'S BIBLE READING:
....
....
....

Make a joyful noise unto the Lord, all the earth:
make a loud noise, and rejoice, and sing praise.
PSALM 98:4

DAY 174   Today's Date: _____

⚲ MY PRAYER FOR TODAY: ....
....
....

MY TAKEAWAY FROM TODAY'S BIBLE READING:
....
....
....

READ:

2 Kings 2–3;
Acts 5:12–28;
Psalm 99

Exalt the Lord our God, and worship at his
holy hill; for the Lord our God is holy.
PSALM 99:9

Today's Date: _____

MY PRAYER FOR TODAY: ....
....
....

MY TAKEAWAY FROM TODAY'S BIBLE READING:
....
....
....

READ:

2 KINGS 4;
ACTS 5:29–6:15;
PSALM 100

We will give ourselves continually to prayer,
and to the ministry of the word.
ACTS 6:4

Today's Date: _____

MY PRAYER FOR TODAY: ....
....
....

READ:

2 KINGS 5:1–6:23;
ACTS 7:1–16;
PSALM 101

MY TAKEAWAY FROM TODAY'S BIBLE READING:
....
....
....

Mine eyes shall be upon the faithful of the land, that they may dwell
with me: he that walketh in a perfect way, he shall serve me.
PSALM 101:6

DAY 177 Today's Date: _____

📍 MY PRAYER FOR TODAY: ....
....
....

READ:

2 Kings 6:24–8:15;
Acts 7:17–36;
Psalm 102:1–7

MY TAKEAWAY FROM TODAY'S BIBLE READING:
....
....
....

Hear my prayer, O Lord, and let my cry come unto thee. Hide not thy face from me in the day when I am in trouble; incline thine ear unto me: in the day when I call answer me speedily.
Psalm 102:1–2

DAY 178 Today's Date: _____

📍 MY PRAYER FOR TODAY: ....
....
....

READ:

2 Kings 8:16–9:37;
Acts 7:37–53;
Psalm 102:8–17

MY TAKEAWAY FROM TODAY'S BIBLE READING:
....
....
....

My days are like a shadow that declineth; and I am withered like grass. But thou, O Lord, shall endure for ever; and thy remembrance unto all generations.
Psalm 102:11–12

Today's Date: _____

MY PRAYER FOR TODAY: ....
....
....

MY TAKEAWAY FROM TODAY'S BIBLE READING:

READ:

2 Kings 10–11;
Acts 7:54–8:8;
Psalm 102:18–28

....
....
....

This shall be written for the generation to come:
and the people which shall be created shall praise the Lord.
Psalm 102:18

Today's Date: _____

MY PRAYER FOR TODAY: ....
....
....

READ:

2 Kings 12–13;
Acts 8:9–40;
Psalm 103:1–9

MY TAKEAWAY FROM TODAY'S BIBLE READING:

....
....
....

I believe that Jesus Christ is the Son of God.
Acts 8:37

DAY 181   Today's Date: _____

MY PRAYER FOR TODAY: ....
....
....

READ:

2 KINGS 14–15;
ACTS 9:1–16;
PSALM 103:10–14

MY TAKEAWAY FROM TODAY'S BIBLE READING:

....
....
....

For he knoweth our frame;
he remembereth that we are dust.
PSALM 103:14

DAY 182   Today's Date: _____

MY PRAYER FOR TODAY: ....
....
....

MY TAKEAWAY FROM TODAY'S BIBLE READING:

....
....
....

READ:

2 KINGS 16–17;
ACTS 9:17–31;
PSALM 103:15–22

The mercy of the LORD is from everlasting to everlasting upon them
that fear him, and his righteousness unto children's children.
PSALM 103:17

Today's Date: _____ **DAY 183**

📍 MY PRAYER FOR TODAY: ....
....
....

MY TAKEAWAY FROM TODAY'S BIBLE READING:
....

READ:

2 KINGS 18:1–19:7;
ACTS 9:32–10:16;
PSALM 104:1–9

....
....

Bless the LORD, O my soul. O LORD my God, thou art
very great; thou art clothed with honour and majesty.
PSALM 104:1

Today's Date: _____ **DAY 184**

📍 MY PRAYER FOR TODAY: ....
....
....

READ:

2 KINGS 19:8–20:21;
ACTS 10:17–33;
PSALM 104:10–23

MY TAKEAWAY FROM TODAY'S BIBLE READING:
....
....
....

He watereth the hills. . .the earth is satisfied with the fruit of thy
works. He causeth the grass to grow for the cattle, and herb for
the service of man: that he may bring forth food out of the earth.
PSALM 104:13–14

DAY 185 Today's Date: _____

📍 MY PRAYER FOR TODAY: ....
....
....

READ:

2 Kings 21:1–22:20;
Acts 10:34–11:18;
Psalm 104:24–30

MY TAKEAWAY FROM TODAY'S BIBLE READING:

....
....
....

*In every nation he that feareth him, and worketh righteousness,
is accepted with him. The word which God sent unto the children
of Israel, preaching peace by Jesus Christ: (he is Lord of all).*
Acts 10:35–36

DAY 186 Today's Date: _____

📍 MY PRAYER FOR TODAY: ....
....
....

MY TAKEAWAY FROM TODAY'S BIBLE READING:

....
....
....

READ:

2 Kings 23;
Acts 11:19–12:17;
Psalm 104:31–35

*I will sing unto the Lord as long as I live: I will sing
praise to my God while I have my being. My meditation
of him shall be sweet: I will be glad in the Lord.*
Psalm 104:33–34

Today's Date: _____

MY PRAYER FOR TODAY: ....
....
....

MY TAKEAWAY FROM TODAY'S BIBLE READING:

....
....
....

READ:

2 Kings 24–25;
Acts 12:18–13:13;
Psalm 105:1–7

O give thanks unto the Lord; call upon his name:
make known his deeds among the people. Sing unto him,
sing psalms unto him: talk ye of all his wondrous works.
Psalm 105:1–2

Today's Date: _____

MY PRAYER FOR TODAY: ....
....
....

READ:

1 Chronicles 1–2;
Acts 13:14–43;
Psalm 105:8–15

MY TAKEAWAY FROM TODAY'S BIBLE READING:

....
....
....

He hath remembered his covenant for ever, the word which he
commanded to a thousand generations. . . . When they were
but a few men in number; yea, very few, and strangers in it.
Psalm 105:8, 12

DAY 189   Today's Date: _____

📍 MY PRAYER FOR TODAY: ....
....
....

READ:

1 CHRONICLES
3:1–5:10;
ACTS 13:44–14:10;
PSALM 105:16–28

MY TAKEAWAY FROM TODAY'S BIBLE READING:

....
....
....

*And the disciples were filled with joy,
and with the Holy Ghost.*
ACTS 13:52

DAY 190   Today's Date: _____

📍 MY PRAYER FOR TODAY: ....
....
....

MY TAKEAWAY FROM TODAY'S BIBLE READING:

....
....
....

READ:

1 CHRONICLES
5:11–6:81;
ACTS 14:11–28;
PSALM 105:29–36

*Ye should turn from these vanities unto the living God, which made
heaven, and earth, and the sea, and all things that are therein.*
ACTS 14:15

Today's Date: _____ **DAY 191**

MY PRAYER FOR TODAY: ....
....
....

MY TAKEAWAY FROM TODAY'S BIBLE READING:

....
....
....

READ:

1 Chronicles 7:1–9:9;
Acts 15:1–18;
Psalm 105:37–45

*And gave them the lands of the heathen: and they inherited
the labour of the people; that they might observe his
statutes, and keep his laws. Praise ye the Lord.*
Psalm 105:44–45

Today's Date: _____ **DAY 192**

MY PRAYER FOR TODAY: ....
....
....

READ:

1 Chronicles
9:10–11:9;
Acts 15:19–41;
Psalm 106:1–12

MY TAKEAWAY FROM TODAY'S BIBLE READING:

....
....
....

*Remember me, O Lord, with the favour that thou bearest unto thy
people: O visit me with thy salvation; that I may see the good of
thy chosen, that I may rejoice in the gladness of thy nation.*
Psalm 106:4–5

DAY 193

Today's Date: _____

📍 MY PRAYER FOR TODAY: ....
....
....

READ:

1 Chronicles
11:10–12:40;
Acts 16:1–15;
Psalm 106:13–27

MY TAKEAWAY FROM TODAY'S BIBLE READING:

....
....
....

*And so were the churches established in
the faith, and increased in number daily.*
Acts 16:5

DAY 194

Today's Date: _____

📍 MY PRAYER FOR TODAY: ....
....
....

MY TAKEAWAY FROM TODAY'S BIBLE READING:

READ:

1 Chronicles 13–15;
Acts 16:16–40;
Psalm 106:28–33

....
....
....

*Believe on the Lord Jesus Christ,
and thou shalt be saved, and thy house.*
Acts 16:31

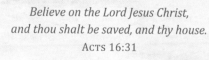

Today's Date: _____

MY PRAYER FOR TODAY: ....
....
....

MY TAKEAWAY FROM TODAY'S BIBLE READING:
....
....
....

READ:

1 Chronicles 16–17;
Acts 17:1–14;
Psalm 106:34–43

This Jesus, whom I preach unto you, is Christ.
Acts 17:3

Today's Date: _____

MY PRAYER FOR TODAY: ....
....
....

READ:

1 Chronicles 18–20;
Acts 17:15–34;
Psalm 106:44–48

MY TAKEAWAY FROM TODAY'S BIBLE READING:
....
....
....

*For in him we live, and move, and have our being; as certain also
of your own poets have said, For we are also his offspring.*
Acts 17:28

DAY 197 Today's Date: _____

MY PRAYER FOR TODAY: ....
....
....

READ:

1 CHRONICLES 21–22;
ACTS 18:1–23;
PSALM 107:1–9

MY TAKEAWAY FROM TODAY'S BIBLE READING:
....
....
....

Oh that men would praise the LORD for his goodness, and for his wonderful works to the children of men! For he satisfieth the longing soul, and filleth the hungry soul with goodness.
PSALM 107:8–9

DAY 198 Today's Date: _____

MY PRAYER FOR TODAY: ....
....
....

MY TAKEAWAY FROM TODAY'S BIBLE READING:
....
....
....

READ:

1 CHRONICLES 23–25;
ACTS 18:24–19:10;
PSALM 107:10–16

They cried unto the LORD in their trouble, and he saved them out of their distresses.
PSALM 107:13

Today's Date: _____

MY PRAYER FOR TODAY: ....
....
....

MY TAKEAWAY FROM TODAY'S BIBLE READING:

READ:

1 Chronicles 26–27;
Acts 19:11–22;
Psalm 107:17–32

....
....

*[The Lord] sent his word, and healed them, and delivered them
from their destructions. Oh that men would praise the Lord for
his goodness, and for his wonderful works to the children of men!*
Psalm 107:20–21

Today's Date: _____

MY PRAYER FOR TODAY: ....
....
....

READ:

1 Chronicles 28–29;
Acts 19:23–41;
Psalm 107:33–38

MY TAKEAWAY FROM TODAY'S BIBLE READING:

....
....
....

*Be strong and of good courage. . .fear not, nor be dismayed:
for the Lord God, even my God, will be with thee;
he will not fail thee, nor forsake thee.*
1 Chronicles 28:20

DAY 201

Today's Date: _____

📍 MY PRAYER FOR TODAY: ....
....
....

READ:

2 Chronicles 1–3;
Acts 20:1–16;
Psalm 107:39–43

MY TAKEAWAY FROM TODAY'S BIBLE READING:
....
....
....

*He poureth contempt upon princes, and causeth them to wander in
the wilderness, where there is no way. Yet setteth he the poor on
high from affliction, and maketh him families like a flock.*
PSALM 107:40–41

DAY 202

Today's Date: _____

📍 MY PRAYER FOR TODAY: ....
....
....

MY TAKEAWAY FROM TODAY'S BIBLE READING:

READ:

2 Chronicles
4:1–6:11;
Acts 20:17–38;
Psalm 108

....
....
....

*Neither count I my life dear unto myself, so that I might finish
my course with joy, and the ministry, which I have received
of the Lord Jesus, to testify the gospel of the grace of God.*
ACTS 20:24

Today's Date: _____   **DAY 203**

⊙ MY PRAYER FOR TODAY: ....
....
....

MY TAKEAWAY FROM TODAY'S BIBLE READING:

....

....

....

READ:

2 CHRONICLES 6:12–
7:10; ACTS 21:1–14;
PSALM 109:1–20

*But will God in very deed dwell with men on the earth?
behold, heaven and the heaven of heavens cannot contain
thee; how much less this house which I have built!*
2 CHRONICLES 6:18

Today's Date: _____   **DAY 204**

⊙ MY PRAYER FOR TODAY: ....
....
....

READ:

2 CHRONICLES 7:11–
9:28; ACTS 21:15–32;
PSALM 109:21–31

MY TAKEAWAY FROM TODAY'S BIBLE READING:

....

....

....

*If my people. . .shall humble themselves, and pray, and seek my
face, and turn from their wicked ways; then will I hear from
heaven, and will forgive their sin, and will heal their land.*
2 CHRONICLES 7:14

DAY 205 Today's Date: _____

📍 MY PRAYER FOR TODAY: ....
....
....

READ:
2 Chronicles
9:29–12:16;
Acts 21:33–22:16;
Psalm 110:1–3

MY TAKEAWAY FROM TODAY'S BIBLE READING:
....
....
....

The God of our fathers hath chosen thee, that thou shouldest know his will, and see that Just One, and shouldest hear the voice of his mouth.
Acts 22:14

DAY 206 Today's Date: _____

📍 MY PRAYER FOR TODAY: ....
....
....

MY TAKEAWAY FROM TODAY'S BIBLE READING:
....
....
....

READ:
2 Chronicles 13–15;
Acts 22:17–23:11;
Psalm 110:4–7

God himself is with us for our captain. . . . O children of Israel, fight ye not against the Lord God of your fathers; for ye shall not prosper.
2 Chronicles 13:12

Today's Date: _____

MY PRAYER FOR TODAY: ....
....
....

MY TAKEAWAY FROM TODAY'S BIBLE READING:
....
....
....

READ:

2 Chronicles 16–17;
Acts 23:12–24:21;
Psalm 111

*For the eyes of the Lord run to and fro throughout
the whole earth, to shew himself strong in the behalf
of them whose heart is perfect toward him.*
2 Chronicles 16:9

Today's Date: _____

MY PRAYER FOR TODAY: ....
....
....

READ:

2 Chronicles 18–19;
Acts 24:22–25:12;
Psalm 112

MY TAKEAWAY FROM TODAY'S BIBLE READING:
....
....
....

*Praise ye the Lord. Blessed is the man that feareth the
Lord, that delighteth greatly in his commandments.*
Psalm 112:1

DAY 209 Today's Date: _____

MY PRAYER FOR TODAY: ....

....

....

READ:

2 Chronicles 20–21;
Acts 25:13–27;
Psalm 113

MY TAKEAWAY FROM TODAY'S BIBLE READING:

....

....

....

*Art not thou our God, who didst drive out the inhabitants
of this land before thy people Israel, and gavest it
to the seed of Abraham thy friend for ever?*
2 Chronicles 20:7

DAY 210 Today's Date: _____

MY PRAYER FOR TODAY: ....

....

....

MY TAKEAWAY FROM TODAY'S BIBLE READING:

....

....

....

READ:

2 Chronicles 22–23;
Acts 26;
Psalm 114

*Tremble, thou earth, at the presence of the Lord, at the
presence of the God of Jacob; which turned the rock into
a standing water, the flint into a fountain of waters.*
Psalm 114:7–8

Today's Date: _____

MY PRAYER FOR TODAY: ....
....
....

MY TAKEAWAY FROM TODAY'S BIBLE READING:

....
....
....

READ:

2 CHRONICLES
24:1–25:16;
ACTS 27:1–20;
PSALM 115:1–10

*Our God is in the heavens: he hath
done whatsoever he hath pleased.*
PSALM 115:3

Today's Date: _____

MY PRAYER FOR TODAY: ....
....
....

READ:

2 CHRONICLES
25:17–27:9;
ACTS 27:21–28:6;
PSALM 115:11–18

MY TAKEAWAY FROM TODAY'S BIBLE READING:

....
....
....

*Be of good cheer: for I believe God,
that it shall be even as it was told me.*
ACTS 27:25

DAY 213 Today's Date: _____

📍 MY PRAYER FOR TODAY: ....
....
....

READ:

2 Chronicles
28:1–29:19;
Acts 28:7–31;
Psalm 116:1–5

MY TAKEAWAY FROM TODAY'S BIBLE READING:

....
....
....

*I love the Lord, because he hath heard my voice and
my supplications. Because he hath inclined his ear unto
me, therefore will I call upon him as long as I live.*
Psalm 116:1–2

DAY 214 Today's Date: _____

📍 MY PRAYER FOR TODAY: ....
....
....

MY TAKEAWAY FROM TODAY'S BIBLE READING:

....
....
....

READ:

2 Chronicles
29:20–30:27;
Romans 1:1–17;
Psalm 116:6–19

*Return unto thy rest, O my soul; for the Lord hath dealt
bountifully with thee. For thou hast delivered my soul from
death, mine eyes from tears, and my feet from falling.*
Psalm 116:7–8

Today's Date: _____

MY PRAYER FOR TODAY: ....
....
....

MY TAKEAWAY FROM TODAY'S BIBLE READING:

....
....
....

READ:

2 CHRONICLES 31–32;
ROMANS 1:18–32;
PSALM 117

Be strong and courageous, be not afraid nor dismayed. . .
with us is the LORD our God to help us, and to fight our battles.
2 CHRONICLES 32:7–8

Today's Date: _____

MY PRAYER FOR TODAY: ....
....
....

READ:

2 CHRONICLES
33:1–34:7;
ROMANS 2;
PSALM 118:1–18

MY TAKEAWAY FROM TODAY'S BIBLE READING:

....
....
....

It is better to trust in the LORD than to put confidence in man. It is
better to trust in the LORD than to put confidence in princes.
PSALM 118:8–9

DAY 217 Today's Date: _____

⊙ MY PRAYER FOR TODAY: ....
....
....

READ:

2 CHRONICLES
34:8–35:19;
ROMANS 3:1–26;
PSALM 118:19–23

MY TAKEAWAY FROM TODAY'S BIBLE READING:

....
....
....

*Even the righteousness of God which is by faith of Jesus Christ unto
all and upon all them that believe: for there is no difference:
for all have sinned, and come short of the glory of God.*
ROMANS 3:22–23

DAY 218 Today's Date: _____

⊙ MY PRAYER FOR TODAY: ....
....
....

MY TAKEAWAY FROM TODAY'S BIBLE READING:

....
....
....

READ:

2 CHRONICLES
35:20–36:23;
ROMANS 3:27–4:25;
PSALM 118:24–29

*This is the day which the LORD hath made;
we will rejoice and be glad in it.*
PSALM 118:24

Today's Date: _____

DAY 219

MY PRAYER FOR TODAY: ....
....
....

MY TAKEAWAY FROM TODAY'S BIBLE READING:
....
....
....

READ:

Ezra 1–3;
Romans 5;
Psalm 119:1–8

*Therefore being justified by faith, we have peace
with God through our Lord Jesus Christ.*
Romans 5:1

Today's Date: _____

DAY 220

MY PRAYER FOR TODAY: ....
....
....

READ:

Ezra 4–5;
Romans 6:1–7:6;
Psalm 119:9–16

MY TAKEAWAY FROM TODAY'S BIBLE READING:
....
....
....

*Thy word have I hid in mine heart,
that I might not sin against thee.*
Psalm 119:11

DAY 221 Today's Date: _____

📍 MY PRAYER FOR TODAY: ....
....
....

READ:

Ezra 6:1–7:26;
Romans 7:7–25;
Psalm 119:17–32

MY TAKEAWAY FROM TODAY'S BIBLE READING:

....
....
....

I thank God through Jesus Christ our Lord. So then with the mind I myself serve the law of God; but with the flesh the law of sin.
ROMANS 7:25

DAY 222 Today's Date: _____

📍 MY PRAYER FOR TODAY: ....
....
....

MY TAKEAWAY FROM TODAY'S BIBLE READING:

....
....
....

READ:

Ezra 7:27–9:4;
Romans 8:1–27;
Psalm 119:33–40

There is therefore now no condemnation to them which are in Christ Jesus, who walk not after the flesh, but after the Spirit.
ROMANS 8:1

Today's Date: .... **DAY 223**

📍 MY PRAYER FOR TODAY: ....
....
....

MY TAKEAWAY FROM TODAY'S BIBLE READING:
....
....
....

READ:

Ezra 9:5–10:44;
Romans 8:28–39;
Psalm 119:41–64

*Nay, in all these things we are more than
conquerors through him that loved us.*
Romans 8:37

Today's Date: .... **DAY 224**

📍 MY PRAYER FOR TODAY: ....
....
....

READ:

Nehemiah 1:1–3:16;
Romans 9:1–18;
Psalm 119:65–72

MY TAKEAWAY FROM TODAY'S BIBLE READING:
....
....
....

I prayed to the God of heaven.
Nehemiah 2:4

DAY 225 Today's Date: _____

MY PRAYER FOR TODAY: ....

....

....

READ:

Nehemiah 3:17–5:13;
Romans 9:19–33;
Psalm 119:73–80

MY TAKEAWAY FROM TODAY'S BIBLE READING:

....

....

....

*Thy hands have made me and fashioned me: give me
understanding, that I may learn thy commandments.*
Psalm 119:73

DAY 226 Today's Date: _____

MY PRAYER FOR TODAY: ....

....

....

MY TAKEAWAY FROM TODAY'S BIBLE READING:

....

....

....

READ:

Nehemiah 5:14–7:73;
Romans 10:1–13;
Psalm 119:81–88

Now therefore, O God, strengthen my hands.
Nehemiah 6:9

Today's Date: _____

MY PRAYER FOR TODAY: ....
....
....

MY TAKEAWAY FROM TODAY'S BIBLE READING:
....
....
....

READ:

NEHEMIAH 8:1–9:5;
ROMANS 10:14–11:24;
PSALM 119:89–104

Unless thy law had been my delights,
I should then have perished in mine affliction.
PSALM 119:92

Today's Date: _____

MY PRAYER FOR TODAY: ....
....
....

READ:

NEHEMIAH 9:6–10:27;
ROMANS 11:25–12:8;
PSALM 119:105–120

MY TAKEAWAY FROM TODAY'S BIBLE READING:
....
....
....

Thy word is a lamp unto my feet,
and a light unto my path.
PSALM 119:105

DAY 229 Today's Date: _____

MY PRAYER FOR TODAY: ....
....
....

READ:

Nehemiah
10:28–12:26;
Romans 12:9–13:7;
Psalm 119:121–128

MY TAKEAWAY FROM TODAY'S BIBLE READING:

....
....
....

Be of the same mind one toward another. Mind not high things, but condescend to men of low estate. Be not wise in your own conceits.
ROMANS 12:16

DAY 230 Today's Date: _____

MY PRAYER FOR TODAY: ....
....
....

MY TAKEAWAY FROM TODAY'S BIBLE READING:

READ:

Nehemiah
12:27–13:31;
Romans 13:8–14:12;
Psalm 119:129–136

....
....
....

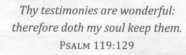

Thy testimonies are wonderful: therefore doth my soul keep them.
PSALM 119:129

Today's Date: _____   DAY 231

MY PRAYER FOR TODAY: ....
....
....

MY TAKEAWAY FROM TODAY'S BIBLE READING:
....
....
....

READ:

Esther 1:1–2:18;
Romans 14:13–15:13;
Psalm 119:137–152

*Now the God of hope fill you with all joy and peace in believing,
that ye may abound in hope, through the power of the Holy Ghost.*
Romans 15:13

Today's Date: _____   DAY 232

MY PRAYER FOR TODAY: ....
....
....

READ:

Esther 2:19–5:14;
Romans 15:14–21;
Psalm 119:153–168

MY TAKEAWAY FROM TODAY'S BIBLE READING:
....
....
....

*Thy word is true from the beginning: and every
one of thy righteous judgments endureth for ever.*
Psalm 119:160

DAY 233

Today's Date: _____

📍 MY PRAYER FOR TODAY: ....
....
....

READ:

Esther 6–8;
Romans 15:22–33;
Psalm 119:169–176

MY TAKEAWAY FROM TODAY'S BIBLE READING:
....
....
....
....

*Let thine hand help me;
for I have chosen thy precepts.*
PSALM 119:173

DAY 234

Today's Date: _____

📍 MY PRAYER FOR TODAY: ....
....
....

MY TAKEAWAY FROM TODAY'S BIBLE READING:
....
....
....

READ:

Esther 9–10;
Romans 16;
Psalms 120–122

*For your obedience is come abroad unto all men. I am
glad therefore on your behalf: but yet I would have you
wise unto that which is good, and simple concerning evil.*
ROMANS 16:19

Today's Date: _____

MY PRAYER FOR TODAY: ....

....

....

MY TAKEAWAY FROM TODAY'S BIBLE READING:

....

....

....

READ:
Job 1–3;
1 Corinthians
1:1–25;
Psalm 123

*And said, Naked came I out of my mother's womb,
and naked shall I return thither: the Lord gave, and the
Lord hath taken away; blessed be the name of the Lord.*
Job 1:21

Today's Date: _____

MY PRAYER FOR TODAY: ....

....

....

READ:
Job 4–6;
1 Corinthians
1:26–2:16;
Psalms 124–125

MY TAKEAWAY FROM TODAY'S BIBLE READING:

....

....

....

*But God hath chosen the foolish things of the world to
confound the wise; and God hath chosen the weak things
of the world to confound the things which are mighty.*
1 Corinthians 1:27

DAY 237 Today's Date: _____

MY PRAYER FOR TODAY: ....
....
....

READ:

Job 7–9;
1 Corinthians 3;
Psalms 126–127

MY TAKEAWAY FROM TODAY'S BIBLE READING:
....
....
....

> *Lo, children are an heritage of the Lord: and the fruit*
> *of the womb is his reward. As arrows are in the hand*
> *of a mighty man; so are children of the youth.*
> Psalm 127:3–4

DAY 238 Today's Date: _____

MY PRAYER FOR TODAY: ....
....
....

MY TAKEAWAY FROM TODAY'S BIBLE READING:
....
....
....

READ:

Job 10–13;
1 Corinthians
4:1–13;
Psalms 128–129

> *For I know nothing by myself; yet am I not*
> *hereby justified: but he that judgeth me is the Lord.*
> 1 Corinthians 4:4

Today's Date: _____

📍 MY PRAYER FOR TODAY: ....
....
....

MY TAKEAWAY FROM TODAY'S BIBLE READING:

....

....

....

READ:
Job 14–16;
1 Corinthians
4:14–5:13;
Psalm 130

I wait for the LORD, my soul doth wait, and in his word do I hope.
My soul waiteth for the Lord more than they that watch for
the morning: I say, more than they that watch for the morning.
PSALM 130:5–6

Today's Date: _____

📍 MY PRAYER FOR TODAY: ....
....
....

READ:

Job 17–20;
1 Corinthians 6;
Psalm 131

MY TAKEAWAY FROM TODAY'S BIBLE READING:

....

....

....

For I know that my redeemer liveth, and that he shall stand
at the latter day upon the earth: and though after my skin
worms destroy this body, yet in my flesh shall I see God.
JOB 19:25–26

DAY 241 Today's Date: _____

MY PRAYER FOR TODAY: ....
....
....

READ:

Job 21–23;
1 Corinthians
7:1–16;
Psalm 132

MY TAKEAWAY FROM TODAY'S BIBLE READING:

....
....
....

*But he knoweth the way that I take: when he
hath tried me, I shall come forth as gold.*
Job 23:10

DAY 242 Today's Date: _____

MY PRAYER FOR TODAY: ....
....
....

MY TAKEAWAY FROM TODAY'S BIBLE READING:

....
....
....

READ:

Job 24–27;
1 Corinthians
7:17–40;
Psalms 133–134

*Behold, how good and how pleasant it
is for brethren to dwell together in unity!*
Psalm 133:1

Today's Date: _____   **DAY 243**

MY PRAYER FOR TODAY: ....
....
....

MY TAKEAWAY FROM TODAY'S BIBLE READING:

....

....

....

READ:

JOB 28–30;
1 CORINTHIANS 8;
PSALM 135

And if any man think that he knoweth any thing,
he knoweth nothing yet as he ought to know.
But if any man love God, the same is known of him.
1 CORINTHIANS 8:2–3

Today's Date: _____   **DAY 244**

MY PRAYER FOR TODAY: ....
....
....

READ:

JOB 31–33;
1 CORINTHIANS 9:1–18;
PSALM 136:1–9

MY TAKEAWAY FROM TODAY'S BIBLE READING:

....

....

....

O give thanks unto the LORD; for he is good:
for his mercy endureth for ever.
PSALM 136:1

DAY 245   Today's Date: _____

📍 MY PRAYER FOR TODAY: ....
....
....

READ:

Job 34–36;
1 Corinthians
9:19–10:13;
Psalm 136:10–26

MY TAKEAWAY FROM TODAY'S BIBLE READING:

....
....
....

To the weak became I as weak, that I might gain the weak:
I am made all things to all men, that I might by all
means save some. And this I do for the gospel's sake.
1 Corinthians 9:22–23

DAY 246   Today's Date: _____

📍 MY PRAYER FOR TODAY: ....
....
....

MY TAKEAWAY FROM TODAY'S BIBLE READING:

READ:

Job 37–39;
1 Corinthians
10:14–11:1;
Psalm 137

....
....
....

Where wast thou when I laid the foundations
of the earth? declare, if thou hast understanding.
Job 38:4

Today's Date: _____ **DAY 247**

📍 MY PRAYER FOR TODAY: ....
....
....

MY TAKEAWAY FROM TODAY'S BIBLE READING:

READ:
Job 40–42;
1 Corinthians
11:2–34;
Psalm 138

....
....
....

Who is he that hideth counsel without knowledge?
therefore have I uttered that I understood not;
things too wonderful for me, which I knew not.
Job 42:3

Today's Date: _____ **DAY 248**

📍 MY PRAYER FOR TODAY: ....
....
....

READ:
Ecclesiastes 1:1–3:15;
1 Corinthians
12:1–26;
Psalm 139:1–6

MY TAKEAWAY FROM TODAY'S BIBLE READING:

....
....
....

O lord, thou hast searched me, and known me.
Thou knowest my downsitting and mine uprising,
thou understandest my thought afar off.
Psalm 139:1–2

DAY 249   Today's Date: _____

📍 MY PRAYER FOR TODAY: ....
....
....

READ:
Ecclesiastes
3:16–6:12;
1 Corinthians
12:27–13:13;
Psalm 139:7–18

MY TAKEAWAY FROM TODAY'S BIBLE READING:
....
....
....

*Thine eyes did see my substance, yet being unperfect; and in
thy book all my members were written, which in continuance
were fashioned, when as yet there was none of them.*
Psalm 139:16

DAY 250   Today's Date: _____

📍 MY PRAYER FOR TODAY: ....
....
....

MY TAKEAWAY FROM TODAY'S BIBLE READING:
....
....
....

READ:
Ecclesiastes
7:1–9:12;
1 Corinthians
14:1–22;
Psalm 139:19–24

*Whatsoever thy hand findeth to do, do it with thy might;
for there is no work, nor device, nor knowledge,
nor wisdom, in the grave, whither thou goest.*
Ecclesiastes 9:10

Today's Date: _____

MY PRAYER FOR TODAY: ....
....
....

MY TAKEAWAY FROM TODAY'S BIBLE READING:
....
....
....

READ:
ECCLESIASTES
9:13–12:14;
1 CORINTHIANS
14:23–15:11;
PSALM 140:1–8

*Fear God, and keep his commandments: for this is the whole
duty of man. For God shall bring every work into judgment,
with every secret thing, whether it be good, or whether it be evil.*
ECCLESIASTES 12:13–14

Today's Date: _____

MY PRAYER FOR TODAY: ....
....
....

READ:

SONG OF SOLOMON 1–4;
1 CORINTHIANS
15:12–34;
PSALM 140:9–13

MY TAKEAWAY FROM TODAY'S BIBLE READING:
....
....
....

If in this life only we have hope in Christ.
1 CORINTHIANS 15:19

DAY 253   Today's Date: _____

📍 MY PRAYER FOR TODAY: ....
....
....

READ:

Song of Solomon 5–8;
1 Corinthians
15:35–58;
Psalm 141

MY TAKEAWAY FROM TODAY'S BIBLE READING:
....
....
....

Set a watch, O Lord, before my mouth;
keep the door of my lips.
Psalm 141:3

DAY 254   Today's Date: _____

📍 MY PRAYER FOR TODAY: ....
....
....

MY TAKEAWAY FROM TODAY'S BIBLE READING:
....
....
....

READ:

Isaiah 1–2;
1 Corinthians 16;
Psalm 142

Wash you, make you clean; put away the evil of your doings. . .
cease to do evil; learn to do well; seek judgment, relieve the
oppressed, judge the fatherless, plead for the widow.
Isaiah 1:16–17

Today's Date: _____

📍 MY PRAYER FOR TODAY: ....
....
....

MY TAKEAWAY FROM TODAY'S BIBLE READING:
....
....
....

READ:
Isaiah 3–5;
2 Corinthians
1:1–11;
Psalm 143:1–6

*Blessed be God, even the Father of our Lord Jesus Christ,
the Father of mercies, and the God of all comfort.*
2 Corinthians 1:3

Today's Date: _____

📍 MY PRAYER FOR TODAY: ....
....
....

READ:
Isaiah 6–8;
2 Corinthians
1:12–2:4;
Psalm 143:7–12

MY TAKEAWAY FROM TODAY'S BIBLE READING:
....
....
....

*Also I heard the voice of the Lord, saying, Whom shall I send,
and who will go for us? Then said I, Here am I; send me.*
Isaiah 6:8

Today's Date: _____

📍 MY PRAYER FOR TODAY: ....
....
....

READ:

Isaiah 9–10;
2 Corinthians
2:5–17;
Psalm 144

MY TAKEAWAY FROM TODAY'S BIBLE READING:

....
....
....

*Lord, what is man, that thou takest knowledge of him!
or the son of man, that thou makest account of him! Man is
like to vanity: his days are as a shadow that passeth away.*
Psalm 144:3–4

DAY 258 Today's Date: _____

📍 MY PRAYER FOR TODAY: ....
....
....

MY TAKEAWAY FROM TODAY'S BIBLE READING:

....
....
....

READ:

Isaiah 11–13;
2 Corinthians 3;
Psalm 145

*Seeing then that we have such hope,
we use great plainness of speech.*
2 Corinthians 3:12

Today's Date: _____

📍 MY PRAYER FOR TODAY: ....
....
....

MY TAKEAWAY FROM TODAY'S BIBLE READING:
....
....
....

READ:

Isaiah 14–16;
2 Corinthians 4;
Psalm 146

*Which made heaven, and earth, the sea, and all that therein is:
which keepeth truth for ever: which executeth judgment for
the oppressed: which giveth food to the hungry.*
Psalm 146:6–7

Today's Date: _____

📍 MY PRAYER FOR TODAY: ....
....
....

READ:

Isaiah 17–19;
2 Corinthians 5;
Psalm 147:1–11

MY TAKEAWAY FROM TODAY'S BIBLE READING:
....
....
....

*We thus judge, that if one died for all, then were all dead: and that
he died for all, that they which live should not henceforth live unto
themselves, but unto him which died for them, and rose again.*
2 Corinthians 5:14–15

DAY 261 Today's Date: _____

MY PRAYER FOR TODAY: ....
....
....

READ:

Isaiah 20–23;
2 Corinthians 6;
Psalm 147:12–20

MY TAKEAWAY FROM TODAY'S BIBLE READING:
....
....
....

For he hath strengthened the bars of thy gates;
he hath blessed thy children within thee.
PSALM 147:13

DAY 262 Today's Date: _____

MY PRAYER FOR TODAY: ....
....
....

MY TAKEAWAY FROM TODAY'S BIBLE READING:
....
....
....

READ:

Isaiah 24:1–26:19;
2 Corinthians 7;
Psalm 148

Praise ye the LORD. Praise ye the LORD from the
heavens: praise him in the heights. Praise ye him,
all his angels: praise ye him, all his hosts.
PSALM 148:1–2

Today's Date: _____

MY PRAYER FOR TODAY: ....
....
....

MY TAKEAWAY FROM TODAY'S BIBLE READING:
....
....
....

READ:

Isaiah 26:20–28:29;
2 Corinthians 8;
Psalms 149–150

> *Let every thing that hath breath*
> *praise the LORD. Praise ye the LORD.*
> Psalm 150:6

Today's Date: _____

MY PRAYER FOR TODAY: ....
....
....

READ:

Isaiah 29–30;
2 Corinthians 9;
Proverbs 1:1–9

MY TAKEAWAY FROM TODAY'S BIBLE READING:
....
....
....

> *Therefore will the LORD wait, that he may be gracious unto*
> *you. . .that he may have mercy upon you: for the LORD is a*
> *God of judgment: blessed are all they that wait for him.*
> Isaiah 30:18

Today's Date: _____

📍 MY PRAYER FOR TODAY: ....
....
....

READ:

Isaiah 31–33;
2 Corinthians 10;
Proverbs 1:10–22

MY TAKEAWAY FROM TODAY'S BIBLE READING:
....
....
....

*Bringing into captivity every
thought to the obedience of Christ.*
2 Corinthians 10:5

Today's Date: _____

📍 MY PRAYER FOR TODAY: ....
....
....

MY TAKEAWAY FROM TODAY'S BIBLE READING:

READ:

Isaiah 34–36;
2 Corinthians 11;
Proverbs 1:23–26

....
....
....

*Say to them that are of a fearful heart, Be strong, fear not:
behold, your God will come with vengeance, even God
with a recompence; he will come and save you.*
Isaiah 35:4

Today's Date: _____

📍 MY PRAYER FOR TODAY: ....
....
....

MY TAKEAWAY FROM TODAY'S BIBLE READING:

READ:

Isaiah 37–38;
2 Corinthians 12:1–
10; Proverbs 1:27–33

....
....
....

But whoso hearkeneth unto me shall dwell safely,
and shall be quiet from fear of evil.
PROVERBS 1:33

Today's Date: _____

📍 MY PRAYER FOR TODAY: ....
....
....

READ:

Isaiah 39–40;
2 Corinthians
12:11–13:14;
Proverbs 2:1–15

MY TAKEAWAY FROM TODAY'S BIBLE READING:

....
....
....

Behold, the Lord GOD will. . .feed his flock like a shepherd:
he shall gather the lambs with his arm, and carry them in
his bosom, and shall gently lead those that are with young.
ISAIAH 40:10–11

DAY 269 Today's Date: _____

📍 MY PRAYER FOR TODAY: ....
....
....

READ:

Isaiah 41–42;
Galatians 1;
Proverbs 2:16–22

MY TAKEAWAY FROM TODAY'S BIBLE READING:

....
....
....

For I the Lord thy God will hold thy right hand,
saying unto thee, Fear not; I will help thee.
Isaiah 41:13

DAY 270 Today's Date: _____

📍 MY PRAYER FOR TODAY: ....
....
....

MY TAKEAWAY FROM TODAY'S BIBLE READING:

READ:

Isaiah 43:1–44:20;
Galatians 2;
Proverbs 3:1–12

....
....
....

My son, forget not my law; but let thine heart keep
my commandments: for length of days, and long life,
and peace, shall they add to thee.
Proverbs 3:1–2

Today's Date: _____   **DAY 271**

📍 MY PRAYER FOR TODAY: ....
....
....

MY TAKEAWAY FROM TODAY'S BIBLE READING:

....

....

....

READ:

Isaiah 44:21–46:13;
Galatians 3:1–18;
Proverbs 3:13–26

*The LORD by wisdom hath founded the earth; by understanding
hath he established the heavens. By his knowledge the depths
are broken up, and the clouds drop down the dew.*
PROVERBS 3:19–20

Today's Date: _____   **DAY 272**

📍 MY PRAYER FOR TODAY: ....
....
....

READ:

Isaiah 47:1–49:13;
Galatians 3:19–29;
Proverbs 3:27–35

MY TAKEAWAY FROM TODAY'S BIBLE READING:

....

....

....

*There is neither Jew nor Greek, there is neither bond
nor free, there is neither male nor female:
for ye are all one in Christ Jesus.*
GALATIANS 3:28

DAY 273 — Today's Date: _____

⚲ MY PRAYER FOR TODAY: ....
....
....

READ:

Isaiah 49:14–51:23;
Galatians 4:1–11;
Proverbs 4:1–19

MY TAKEAWAY FROM TODAY'S BIBLE READING:
....
....
....

The path of the just is as the shining light,
that shineth more and more unto the perfect day.
PROVERBS 4:18

DAY 274 — Today's Date: _____

⚲ MY PRAYER FOR TODAY: ....
....
....

MY TAKEAWAY FROM TODAY'S BIBLE READING:

READ:

Isaiah 52–54;
Galatians 4:12–31;
Proverbs 4:20–27

....
....
....

Keep thy heart with all diligence;
for out of it are the issues of life.
PROVERBS 4:23

Today's Date: _____

MY PRAYER FOR TODAY: ....
....
....

MY TAKEAWAY FROM TODAY'S BIBLE READING:
....
....
....

READ:

Isaiah 55–57;
Galatians 5;
Proverbs 5:1–14

Stand fast therefore in the liberty wherewith Christ hath made us free,
and be not entangled again with the yoke of bondage.
GALATIANS 5:1

Today's Date: _____

MY PRAYER FOR TODAY: ....
....
....

READ:

Isaiah 58–59;
Galatians 6;
Proverbs 5:15–23

MY TAKEAWAY FROM TODAY'S BIBLE READING:
....
....
....

Then shalt thou call, and the LORD shall answer;
thou shalt cry, and he shall say, Here I am.
ISAIAH 58:9

DAY 277 Today's Date: _____

📍 MY PRAYER FOR TODAY: ....
....
....

READ:

Isaiah 60–62;
Ephesians 1;
Proverbs 6:1–5

MY TAKEAWAY FROM TODAY'S BIBLE READING:
....
....
....

*According as he hath chosen us in him before the foundation
of the world, that we should be holy and without blame before
him in love. . .according to the good pleasure of his will.*
Ephesians 1:4–5

DAY 278 Today's Date: _____

📍 MY PRAYER FOR TODAY: ....
....
....

MY TAKEAWAY FROM TODAY'S BIBLE READING:
....
....
....

READ:

Isaiah 63:1–65:16;
Ephesians 2;
Proverbs 6:6–19

*That in the ages to come he might shew the exceeding riches
of his grace in his kindness toward us through Christ Jesus.*
Ephesians 2:7

Today's Date: _____

MY PRAYER FOR TODAY: ....
....
....

MY TAKEAWAY FROM TODAY'S BIBLE READING:

READ:

ISAIAH 65:17–66:24;
EPHESIANS 3:1–4:16;
PROVERBS 6:20–26

....
....
....

And to know the love of Christ, which passeth knowledge,
that ye might be filled with all the fulness of God.
EPHESIANS 3:19

Today's Date: _____

MY PRAYER FOR TODAY: ....
....
....

READ:

JEREMIAH 1–2;
EPHESIANS 4:17–32;
PROVERBS 6:27–35

MY TAKEAWAY FROM TODAY'S BIBLE READING:

....
....
....

Before I formed thee in the belly I knew thee; and before
thou camest forth out of the womb I sanctified thee,
and I ordained thee a prophet unto the nations.
JEREMIAH 1:5

DAY 281   Today's Date: _____

📍 MY PRAYER FOR TODAY: ....
....
....

READ:

Jeremiah 3:1–4:22;
Ephesians 5;
Proverbs 7:1–5

MY TAKEAWAY FROM TODAY'S BIBLE READING:
....
....
....

*My son, keep my words, and lay up my commandments with thee. Keep
my commandments, and live; and my law as the apple of thine eye.*
Proverbs 7:1–2

DAY 282   Today's Date: _____

📍 MY PRAYER FOR TODAY: ....
....
....

MY TAKEAWAY FROM TODAY'S BIBLE READING:
....
....
....

READ:

Jeremiah 4:23–5:31;
Ephesians 6;
Proverbs 7:6–27

*For we wrestle not against flesh and blood, but against
principalities, against powers, against the rulers of the darkness
of this world, against spiritual wickedness in high places.*
Ephesians 6:12

Today's Date: _____

DAY 283

📍 MY PRAYER FOR TODAY: ....
....
....

MY TAKEAWAY FROM TODAY'S BIBLE READING:
....
....
....

READ:

JEREMIAH 6:1–7:26;
PHILIPPIANS 1:1–26;
PROVERBS 8:1–11

Being confident of this very thing, that he which hath begun a good work in you will perform it until the day of Jesus Christ.
PHILIPPIANS 1:6

Today's Date: _____

DAY 284

📍 MY PRAYER FOR TODAY: ....
....
....

READ:

JEREMIAH 7:27–9:16;
PHILIPPIANS 1:27–2:18;
PROVERBS 8:12–21

MY TAKEAWAY FROM TODAY'S BIBLE READING:
....
....
....

Do all things without murmurings and disputings: that ye may be blameless and harmless. . .in the midst of a crooked and perverse nation, among whom ye shine as lights in the world.
PHILIPPIANS 2:14–15

DAY 285   Today's Date: _____

📍 MY PRAYER FOR TODAY: ....
....
....

READ:

Jeremiah 9:17–11:17;
Philippians 2:19–30;
Proverbs 8:22–36

MY TAKEAWAY FROM TODAY'S BIBLE READING:
....
....
....

> *Let not the wise man glory in his wisdom, neither let the mighty*
> *man glory in his might. . .but let him that glorieth glory in this,*
> *that he understandeth and knoweth me, that I am the Lord.*
> Jeremiah 9:23–24

DAY 286   Today's Date: _____

📍 MY PRAYER FOR TODAY: ....
....
....

MY TAKEAWAY FROM TODAY'S BIBLE READING:
....
....
....

READ:

Jeremiah
11:18–13:27;
Philippians 3;
Proverbs 9:1–6

> *And be found in him, not having mine own righteousness,*
> *which is of the law, but that which is through the faith*
> *of Christ, the righteousness which is of God by faith.*
> Philippians 3:9

Today's Date: _____   **DAY 287**

MY PRAYER FOR TODAY: ....
....
....

MY TAKEAWAY FROM TODAY'S BIBLE READING:

....
....
....

READ:

Jeremiah 14–15;
Philippians 4;
Proverbs 9:7–18

*Be careful for nothing; but in every thing by prayer and supplication
with thanksgiving let your requests be made known unto God.*
Philippians 4:6

Today's Date: _____   **DAY 288**

MY PRAYER FOR TODAY: ....
....
....

READ:

Jeremiah 16–17;
Colossians 1:1–23;
Proverbs 10:1–5

MY TAKEAWAY FROM TODAY'S BIBLE READING:

....
....
....

*We also, since the day we heard it, do not cease to pray for you,
and to desire that ye might be filled with the knowledge
of his will in all wisdom and spiritual understanding.*
Colossians 1:9

DAY 289

Today's Date: _____

📍 MY PRAYER FOR TODAY: ....
....
....

READ:

Jeremiah 18:1–20:6;
Colossians 1:24–2:15;
Proverbs 10:6–14

❤️ MY TAKEAWAY FROM TODAY'S BIBLE READING:
....
....
....

*Wise men lay up knowledge: but the
mouth of the foolish is near destruction.*
PROVERBS 10:14

DAY 290

Today's Date: _____

📍 MY PRAYER FOR TODAY: ....
....
....

MY TAKEAWAY FROM TODAY'S BIBLE READING:
....
....
....

READ:

Jeremiah 20:7–22:19;
Colossians 2:16–3:4;
Proverbs 10:15–26

*If ye then be risen with Christ, seek those things which are
above, where Christ sitteth on the right hand of God. Set your
affection on things above, not on things on the earth.*
COLOSSIANS 3:1–2

Today's Date: _____

MY PRAYER FOR TODAY: ....
....
....

MY TAKEAWAY FROM TODAY'S BIBLE READING:
....
....
....

READ:

JEREMIAH
22:20–23:40;
COLOSSIANS 3:5–4:1;
PROVERBS 10:27–32

*And let the peace of God rule in your hearts, to the
which also ye are called in one body; and be ye thankful.*
COLOSSIANS 3:15

Today's Date: _____

DAY 292

MY PRAYER FOR TODAY: ....
....
....

READ:

JEREMIAH 24–25;
COLOSSIANS 4:2–18;
PROVERBS 11:1–11

MY TAKEAWAY FROM TODAY'S BIBLE READING:
....
....
....

*And I will give them an heart to know me, that I am the
LORD: and they shall be my people, and I will be their God:
for they shall return unto me with their whole heart.*
JEREMIAH 24:7

DAY 293 Today's Date: _____

📍 MY PRAYER FOR TODAY: ....
....
....

READ:
JEREMIAH 26–27;
1 THESSALONIANS
1:1–2:8;
PROVERBS 11:12–21

MY TAKEAWAY FROM TODAY'S BIBLE READING:
....
....
....

*A talebearer revealeth secrets: but he that
is of a faithful spirit concealeth the matter.*
PROVERBS 11:13

DAY 294 Today's Date: _____

📍 MY PRAYER FOR TODAY: ....
....
....

MY TAKEAWAY FROM TODAY'S BIBLE READING:
....
....
....

READ:
JEREMIAH 28–29;
1 THESSALONIANS
2:9–3:13;
PROVERBS 11:22–26

*And the Lord make you to increase and abound in love one toward
another, and toward all men, even as we do toward you: to the
end he may stablish your hearts unblameable in holiness.*
1 THESSALONIANS 3:12–13

Today's Date: _____   **DAY 295**

MY PRAYER FOR TODAY: ....
....
....

MY TAKEAWAY FROM TODAY'S BIBLE READING:

READ:
JEREMIAH 30:1–31:22;
1 THESSALONIANS
4:1–5:11;
PROVERBS 11:27–31

....
....
....

The LORD hath appeared of old unto me, saying,
Yea, I have loved thee with an everlasting love:
therefore with lovingkindness have I drawn thee.
JEREMIAH 31:3

Today's Date: _____   **DAY 296**

MY PRAYER FOR TODAY: ....
....
....

READ:
JEREMIAH 31:23–32:35;
1 THESSALONIANS
5:12–28;
PROVERBS 12:1–14

MY TAKEAWAY FROM TODAY'S BIBLE READING:

....
....
....

Faithful is he that calleth you,
who also will do it.
1 THESSALONIANS 5:24

DAY 297

Today's Date:

⊙ MY PRAYER FOR TODAY: ....
....
....

READ:

Jeremiah 32:36–34:7;
2 Thessalonians 1–2;
Proverbs 12:15–20

MY TAKEAWAY FROM TODAY'S BIBLE READING:
....
....
....

*Call unto me, and I will answer thee, and show thee
great and mighty things, which thou knowest not.*
Jeremiah 33:3

DAY 298

Today's Date: _____

⊙ MY PRAYER FOR TODAY: ....
....
....

MY TAKEAWAY FROM TODAY'S BIBLE READING:
....
....
....

READ:

Jeremiah 34:8–36:10;
2 Thessalonians 3;
Proverbs 12:21–28

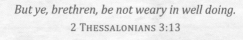

But ye, brethren, be not weary in well doing.
2 Thessalonians 3:13

Today's Date: _____   **DAY 299**

📍 MY PRAYER FOR TODAY: ....
....
....

MY TAKEAWAY FROM TODAY'S BIBLE READING:

....
....
....

READ:

JEREMIAH
36:11–38:13;
1 TIMOTHY 1:1–17;
PROVERBS 13:1–4

*He that keepeth his mouth keepeth his life: but he
that openeth wide his lips shall have destruction.*
PROVERBS 13:3

Today's Date: _____   **DAY 300**

📍 MY PRAYER FOR TODAY: ....
....
....

READ:

JEREMIAH 38:14–40:6;
1 TIMOTHY 1:18–3:13;
PROVERBS 13:5–13

MY TAKEAWAY FROM TODAY'S BIBLE READING:

....
....
....

*There is that maketh himself rich, yet hath nothing:
there is that maketh himself poor, yet hath great riches.*
PROVERBS 13:7

DAY 301 Today's Date: _____

📍 MY PRAYER FOR TODAY: ....

....

....

READ:

Jeremiah 40:7–42:22;
1 Timothy 3:14–4:10;
Proverbs 13:14–21

MY TAKEAWAY FROM TODAY'S BIBLE READING:

....

....

....

*For bodily exercise profiteth little: but godliness is
profitable unto all things, having promise of the
life that now is, and of that which is to come.*
1 Timothy 4:8

DAY 302 Today's Date: _____

📍 MY PRAYER FOR TODAY: ....

....

....

MY TAKEAWAY FROM TODAY'S BIBLE READING:

....

....

....

READ:

Jeremiah 43–44;
1 Timothy 4:11–5:16;
Proverbs 13:22–25

But she that liveth in pleasure is dead while she liveth.
1 Timothy 5:6

Today's Date: _____ **DAY 303**

⊙ MY PRAYER FOR TODAY: ....

....

....

MY TAKEAWAY FROM TODAY'S BIBLE READING:

....

....

....

READ:

Jeremiah 45–47;
1 Timothy 5:17–6:21;
Proverbs 14:1–6

> *But godliness with contentment is great gain. For we brought nothing into this world, and it is certain we can carry nothing out. And having food and raiment let us be therewith content.*
> 1 Timothy 6:6–8

Today's Date: _____ **DAY 304**

⊙ MY PRAYER FOR TODAY: ....

....

....

READ:

Jeremiah 48:1–49:6;
2 Timothy 1;
Proverbs 14:7–22

MY TAKEAWAY FROM TODAY'S BIBLE READING:

....

....

....

> *But is now made manifest by the appearing of our Saviour Jesus Christ, who hath abolished death, and hath brought life and immortality to light through the gospel.*
> 2 Timothy 1:10

DAY 305 Today's Date: _____

📍 MY PRAYER FOR TODAY: ....
....
....

READ:

Jeremiah 49:7–50:16;
2 Timothy 2;
Proverbs 14:23–27

MY TAKEAWAY FROM TODAY'S BIBLE READING:
....
....
....

> *In the fear of the LORD s strong confidence: and his*
> *children shall have a place of refuge. The fear of the LORD*
> *is a fountain of life, to depart from the snares of death.*
> PROVERBS 14:26–27

DAY 306 Today's Date: _____

📍 MY PRAYER FOR TODAY: ....
....
....

MY TAKEAWAY FROM TODAY'S BIBLE READING:

READ:

Jeremiah
50:17–51:14;
2 Timothy 3;
Proverbs 14:28–35

....
....
....

> *Their Redeemer is strong; the LORD of hosts is his name:*
> *he shall throughly plead their cause, that he may give rest*
> *to the land, and disquiet the inhabitants of Babylon.*
> JEREMIAH 50:34

Today's Date: _____

MY PRAYER FOR TODAY: ....
....
....

MY TAKEAWAY FROM TODAY'S BIBLE READING:
....
....
....

READ:

JEREMIAH 51:15–64;
2 TIMOTHY 4;
PROVERBS 15:1–9

*Notwithstanding the Lord stood with me,
and strengthened me.*
2 TIMOTHY 4:17

Today's Date: _____

MY PRAYER FOR TODAY: ....
....
....

READ:

JEREMIAH 52–
LAMENTATIONS 1;
TITUS 1:1–9;
PROVERBS 15:10–17

MY TAKEAWAY FROM TODAY'S BIBLE READING:
....
....
....

*In hope of eternal life, which God, that cannot lie,
promised before the world began.*
TITUS 1:2

DAY 309   Today's Date: _____

📍 MY PRAYER FOR TODAY: ....

....

....

READ:

Lamentations
2:1–3:38;
Titus 1:10–2:15;
Proverbs 15:18–26

MY TAKEAWAY FROM TODAY'S BIBLE READING:

....

....

....

It is of the LORD's mercies that we are not consumed,
because his compassions fail not. They are new
every morning: great is thy faithfulness.
LAMENTATIONS 3:22–23

DAY 310   Today's Date: _____

📍 MY PRAYER FOR TODAY: ....

....

....

MY TAKEAWAY FROM TODAY'S BIBLE READING:

....

....

....

READ:

Lamentations
3:39–5:22;
Titus 3;
Proverbs 15:27–33

The heart of the righteous studieth to answer:
but the mouth of the wicked poureth out evil things.
PROVERBS 15:28

Today's Date: _____

MY PRAYER FOR TODAY: ....
....
....

MY TAKEAWAY FROM TODAY'S BIBLE READING:

....
....
....

READ:

EZEKIEL 1:1–3:21;
PHILEMON;
PROVERBS 16:1–9

A man's heart deviseth his way:
but the LORD directeth his steps.
PROVERBS 16:9

Today's Date: _____

MY PRAYER FOR TODAY: ....
....
....

READ:

EZEKIEL 3:22–5:17;
HEBREWS 1:1–2:4;
PROVERBS 16:10–21

MY TAKEAWAY FROM TODAY'S BIBLE READING:

....
....
....

How shall we escape, if we neglect so great salvation;
which at the first began to be spoken by the Lord,
and was confirmed unto us by them that heard him?
HEBREWS 2:3

DAY 313   Today's Date: _____

📍 MY PRAYER FOR TODAY: ....
....
....

READ:

Ezekiel 6–7;
Hebrews 2:5–18;
Proverbs 16:22–33

MY TAKEAWAY FROM TODAY'S BIBLE READING:
....
....
....

*The hoary head is a crown of glory,
if it be found in the way of righteousness.*
PROVERBS 16:31

DAY 314   Today's Date: _____

📍 MY PRAYER FOR TODAY: ....
....
....

MY TAKEAWAY FROM TODAY'S BIBLE READING:
....
....
....

READ:

Ezekiel 8–10;
Hebrews 3:1–4:3;
Proverbs 17:1–5

*For every house is builded by some man;
but he that built all things is God.*
HEBREWS 3:4

Today's Date: _____ **DAY 315**

📍 MY PRAYER FOR TODAY: ....
....
....

MY TAKEAWAY FROM TODAY'S BIBLE READING:
....
....
....

READ:

EZEKIEL 11–12;
HEBREWS 4:4–5:10;
PROVERBS 17:6–12

Let us therefore come boldly unto the throne of grace, that we may obtain mercy, and find grace to help in time of need.
HEBREWS 4:16

Today's Date: _____ **DAY 316**

📍 MY PRAYER FOR TODAY: ....
....
....

READ:

EZEKIEL 13–14;
HEBREWS 5:11–6:20;
PROVERBS 17:13–22

MY TAKEAWAY FROM TODAY'S BIBLE READING:
....
....
....

Which hope we have as an anchor of the soul, both sure and stedfast, and which entereth into that within the veil.
HEBREWS 6:19

DAY 317   Today's Date: _____

📍 MY PRAYER FOR TODAY: ....

....

....

READ:

Ezekiel 15:1–16:43;
Hebrews 7;
Proverbs 17:23–28

MY TAKEAWAY FROM TODAY'S BIBLE READING:

....

....

....

*He that hath knowledge spareth his words: and a man
of understanding is of an excellent spirit. . .and he that
shutteth his lips is esteemed a man of understanding.*
PROVERBS 17:27–28

DAY 318   Today's Date: _____

📍 MY PRAYER FOR TODAY: ....

....

....

....

MY TAKEAWAY FROM TODAY'S BIBLE READING:

....

....

....

READ:

Ezekiel 16:44–17:24;
Hebrews 8:1–9:10;
Proverbs 18:1–7

*The words of a man's mouth are as deep waters,
and the wellspring of wisdom as a flowing brook.*
PROVERBS 18:4

Today's Date: _____

MY PRAYER FOR TODAY:..
....
....

MY TAKEAWAY FROM TODAY'S BIBLE READING:

....
....
....

READ:

Ezekiel 18–19;
Hebrews 9:11–28;
Proverbs 18:8–17

> *Yet ye say, The way of the LORD is not equal. Hear now, O house of*
> *Israel; Is not my way equal? are not your ways unequal?*
> EZEKIEL 18:25

Today's Date: _____

MY PRAYER FOR TODAY: ....
....
....

READ:

Ezekiel 20;
Hebrews 10:1–25;
Proverbs 18:18–24

MY TAKEAWAY FROM TODAY'S BIBLE READING:

....
....
....

> *A man that hath friends must shew himself friendly:*
> *and there is a friend that sticketh closer than a brother.*
> PROVERBS 18:24

DAY 321　Today's Date: _____

📍 MY PRAYER FOR TODAY: ....
....
....

READ:

Ezekiel 21–22;
Hebrews 10:26–39;
Proverbs 19:1–8

MY TAKEAWAY FROM TODAY'S BIBLE READING:
....
....
....

*He that getteth wisdom loveth his own soul:
he that keepeth understanding shall find good.*
PROVERBS 19:8

DAY 322　Today's Date: _____

📍 MY PRAYER FOR TODAY: ....
....
....

MY TAKEAWAY FROM TODAY'S BIBLE READING:
....
....
....

READ:

Ezekiel 23;
Hebrews 11:1–31;
Proverbs 19:9–14

*For they that say such things declare plainly that they seek
a country. . . . But now they desire a better country, that is,
an heavenly: wherefore God is not ashamed to be called their God.*
HEBREWS 11:14, 16

Today's Date: _____

DAY 323

MY PRAYER FOR TODAY: ....
....
....

MY TAKEAWAY FROM TODAY'S BIBLE READING:
....
....
....

READ:

Ezekiel 24–26;
Hebrews 11:32–40;
Proverbs 19:15–21

He that hath pity upon the poor lendeth unto the LORD;
and that which he hath given will he pay him again.
PROVERBS 19:17

Today's Date: _____

DAY 324

MY PRAYER FOR TODAY: ....
....
....

READ:

Ezekiel 27–28;
Hebrews 12:1–13;
Proverbs 19:22–29

MY TAKEAWAY FROM TODAY'S BIBLE READING:
....
....
....

The fear of the LORD tendeth to life: and he that hath
it shall abide satisfied; he shall not be visited with evil.
PROVERBS 19:23

DAY 325   Today's Date: _____

📍 MY PRAYER FOR TODAY: ....
....
....

READ:

Ezekiel 29–30;
Hebrews 12:14–29;
Proverbs 20:1–18

MY TAKEAWAY FROM TODAY'S BIBLE READING:

....
....
....
....

*Most men will proclaim every one his own
goodness: but a faithful man who can find?*
PROVERBS 20:6

DAY 326   Today's Date: _____

📍 MY PRAYER FOR TODAY: ....
....
....

MY TAKEAWAY FROM TODAY'S BIBLE READING:

....
....
....

READ:

Ezekiel 31–32;
Hebrews 13;
Proverbs 20:19–24

*Say not thou, I will recompense evil;
but wait on the LORD, and he shall save thee.*
PROVERBS 20:22

Today's Date: _____

DAY 327

📍 MY PRAYER FOR TODAY: ....

....

....

MY TAKEAWAY FROM TODAY'S BIBLE READING:

....

....

....

READ:

Ezekiel 33:1–34:10;
James 1;
Proverbs 20:25–30

Pure religion and undefiled before God and the Father is this,
to visit the fatherless and widows in their affliction,
and to keep himself unspotted from the world.
JAMES 1:27

Today's Date: _____

DAY 328

📍 MY PRAYER FOR TODAY: ....

....

....

READ:

Ezekiel 34:11–36:15;
James 2;
Proverbs 21:1–8

MY TAKEAWAY FROM TODAY'S BIBLE READING:

....

....

....

Faith, if it hath not works,
is dead, being alone.
JAMES 2:17

DAY 329 Today's Date: _____

📍 MY PRAYER FOR TODAY: ....
....
....

READ:

Ezekiel 36:16–37:28;
James 3;
Proverbs 21:9–18

MY TAKEAWAY FROM TODAY'S BIBLE READING:
....
....
....

*And shall put my spirit in you, and ye shall live, and I shall
place you in your own land: then shall ye know that I the
LORD have spoken it, and performed it, saith the LORD.*
Ezekiel 37:14

DAY 330 Today's Date: _____

📍 MY PRAYER FOR TODAY: ....
....
....

MY TAKEAWAY FROM TODAY'S BIBLE READING:

READ:

Ezekiel 38–39;
James 4:1–5:6;
Proverbs 21:19–24

....
....
....

*He that followeth after righteousness and mercy
findeth life, righteousness, and honour.*
Proverbs 21:21

Today's Date: _____

🔖 MY PRAYER FOR TODAY: ....
....
....

MY TAKEAWAY FROM TODAY'S BIBLE READING:
....
....
....

READ:

EZEKIEL 40;
JAMES 5:7–20;
PROVERBS 21:25–31

Be ye also patient; stablish your hearts:
for the coming of the Lord draweth nigh.
JAMES 5:8

Today's Date: _____

MY PRAYER FOR TODAY: ....
....
....

READ:

EZEKIEL 41:1–43:12;
1 PETER 1:1–12;
PROVERBS 22:1–9

MY TAKEAWAY FROM TODAY'S BIBLE READING:
....
....
....

An inheritance incorruptible, and undefiled, and that fadeth
not away, reserved in heaven for you, who are kept by the
power of God. . .ready to be revealed in the last time.
1 PETER 1:4–5

DAY 333 Today's Date: _____

📍 MY PRAYER FOR TODAY: ....

....

....

READ:

Ezekiel 43:13–44:31;
1 Peter 1:13–2:3;
Proverbs 22:10–23

MY TAKEAWAY FROM TODAY'S BIBLE READING:

....

....

....

*But as he which hath called you is holy, so be ye holy in all manner of
conversation; because it is written, Be ye holy; for I am holy.*
1 Peter 1:15–16

DAY 334 Today's Date: _____

📍 MY PRAYER FOR TODAY: ....

....

....

MY TAKEAWAY FROM TODAY'S BIBLE READING:

....

....

....

READ:

Ezekiel 45–46;
1 Peter 2:4–17;
Proverbs 22:24–29

*Honour all men. Love the brotherhood.
Fear God. Honour the king.*
1 Peter 2:17

Today's Date: _____   **DAY 335**

📍 MY PRAYER FOR TODAY: ....
....
....

MY TAKEAWAY FROM TODAY'S BIBLE READING:

....

....

....

READ:

EZEKIEL 47–48;
1 PETER 2:18–3:7;
PROVERBS 23:1–9

> *For as he thinketh in his heart, so is he.*
> PROVERBS 23:7

Today's Date: _____   **DAY 336**

📍 MY PRAYER FOR TODAY: ....
....
....

READ:

DANIEL 1:1–2:23;
1 PETER 3:8–4:19;
PROVERBS 23:10–16

MY TAKEAWAY FROM TODAY'S BIBLE READING:

....

....

....

> *Finally, be ye all of one mind, having compassion one of another,*
> *love as brethren, be pitiful, be courteous: not rendering evil*
> *for evil, or railing for railing: but contrariwise blessing.*
> 1 PETER 3:8–9

DAY 337 Today's Date: _____

MY PRAYER FOR TODAY: ....
....
....

READ:

Daniel 2:24–3:30;
1 Peter 5;
Proverbs 23:17–25

MY TAKEAWAY FROM TODAY'S BIBLE READING:
....
....
....

Casting all your care upon him;
for he careth for you.
1 Peter 5:7

DAY 338 Today's Date: _____

MY PRAYER FOR TODAY: ....
....
....

MY TAKEAWAY FROM TODAY'S BIBLE READING:
....
....
....

READ:

Daniel 4;
2 Peter 1;
Proverbs 23:26–35

I blessed the most High, and I praised and honoured him
that liveth for ever, whose dominion is an everlasting
dominion, and his kingdom is from generation to generation.
Daniel 4:34

Today's Date: _____   **DAY 339**

MY PRAYER FOR TODAY: ....
....
....

MY TAKEAWAY FROM TODAY'S BIBLE READING:

....

....

....

READ:

Daniel 5;
2 Peter 2;
Proverbs 24:1–18

*Through wisdom is an house builded; and by understanding
it is established: and by knowledge shall the chambers
be filled with all precious and pleasant riches.*
Proverbs 24:3–4

Today's Date: _____   **DAY 340**

MY PRAYER FOR TODAY: ....
....
....

READ:

Daniel 6:1–7:14;
2 Peter 3;
Proverbs 24:19–27

MY TAKEAWAY FROM TODAY'S BIBLE READING:

....

....

....

*Beloved, be not ignorant of this one thing, that one day is with the
Lord as a thousand years, and a thousand years as one day.*
2 Peter 3:8

DAY 341 Today's Date: _____

MY PRAYER FOR TODAY: ....
....
....

READ:

Daniel 7:15–8:27;
1 John 1:1–2:17;
Proverbs 24:28–34

MY TAKEAWAY FROM TODAY'S BIBLE READING:
....
....
....

*If we say that we have no sin, we deceive ourselves, and the truth
is not in us. If we confess our sins, he is faithful and just to forgive
us our sins, and to cleanse us from all unrighteousness.*
1 John 1:8–9

DAY 342 Today's Date: _____

MY PRAYER FOR TODAY: ....
....
....

MY TAKEAWAY FROM TODAY'S BIBLE READING:
....
....
....

READ:

Daniel 9–10;
1 John 2:18–29;
Proverbs 25:1–12

*Therefore hath the Lord watched upon the evil, and brought
it upon us: for the Lord our God is righteous in all his
works which he doeth: for we obeyed not his voice.*
Daniel 9:14

Today's Date: _____

MY PRAYER FOR TODAY: ....
....
....

MY TAKEAWAY FROM TODAY'S BIBLE READING:
....

READ:

DANIEL 11–12;
1 JOHN 3:1–12;
PROVERBS 25:13–17

....
....

*Behold, what manner of love the Father hath bestowed
upon us, that we should be called the sons of God: therefore
the world knoweth us not, because it knew him not.*
1 JOHN 3:1

Today's Date: _____

MY PRAYER FOR TODAY: ....
....
....

READ:

HOSEA 1–3;
1 JOHN 3:13–4:16;
PROVERBS 25:18–28

MY TAKEAWAY FROM TODAY'S BIBLE READING:
....
....
....

*And I will betroth thee unto me for ever. . .in righteousness. . .
judgment, and in lovingkindness, and in mercies. I will even betroth
thee unto me in faithfulness: and thou shalt know the LORD.*
HOSEA 2:19–20

DAY 345 Today's Date: _____

⊙ MY PRAYER FOR TODAY: ....
....
....

READ:

Hosea 4–6;
1 John 4:17–5:21;
Proverbs 26:1–16

MY TAKEAWAY FROM TODAY'S BIBLE READING:
....
....
....

*Who is he that overcometh the world, but he
that believeth that Jesus is the Son of God?*
1 John 5:5

DAY 346 Today's Date: _____

⊙ MY PRAYER FOR TODAY: ....
....
....

MY TAKEAWAY FROM TODAY'S BIBLE READING:

READ:

Hosea 7–10;
2 John;
Proverbs 26:17–21

....
....
....

*I rejoiced greatly that I found of thy children walking in truth,
as we have received a commandment from the Father.*
2 John 4

Today's Date: _____   **DAY 347**

MY PRAYER FOR TODAY: ....
....
....

MY TAKEAWAY FROM TODAY'S BIBLE READING:

....

....

....

READ:

HOSEA 11–14;
3 JOHN;
PROVERBS 26:22–27:9

Beloved, follow not that which is evil, but that which is good. He that doeth good is of God: but he that doeth evil hath not seen God.
3 JOHN 1:11

Today's Date: _____   **DAY 348**

MY PRAYER FOR TODAY: ....
....
....

READ:

JOEL 1:1–2:17;
JUDE;
PROVERBS 27:10–17

MY TAKEAWAY FROM TODAY'S BIBLE READING:

....

....

....

To the only wise God our Saviour, be glory and majesty, dominion and power, both now and ever. Amen.
JUDE 1:25

DAY 349 Today's Date: _____

📍 MY PRAYER FOR TODAY: ....
....
....

READ:

Joel 2:18–3:21;
Revelation 1:1–2:11;
Proverbs 27:18–27

MY TAKEAWAY FROM TODAY'S BIBLE READING:
....
....
....

*I am Alpha and Omega, the beginning and the ending, saith the Lord,
which is, and which was, and which is to come, the Almighty.*
REVELATION 1:8

DAY 350 Today's Date: _____

📍 MY PRAYER FOR TODAY: ....
....
....

MY TAKEAWAY FROM TODAY'S BIBLE READING:
....
....
....

READ:

Amos 1:1–4:5;
Revelation 2:12–29;
Proverbs 28:1–8

*Better is the poor that walketh in his uprightness,
than he that is perverse in his ways, though he be rich.*
PROVERBS 28:6

Today's Date: _____ **DAY 351**

⟟ MY PRAYER FOR TODAY: ....

....

....

MY TAKEAWAY FROM TODAY'S BIBLE READING:

....

....

....

READ:

Amos 4:6–6:14;
Revelation 3;
Proverbs 28:9–16

*Because thou sayest, I am rich, and increased
with goods, and have need of nothing.*
REVELATION 3:17

Today's Date: _____ **DAY 352**

⟟ MY PRAYER FOR TODAY: ....

....

....

READ:

Amos 7–9;
Revelation 4:1–5:5;
Proverbs 28:17–24

MY TAKEAWAY FROM TODAY'S BIBLE READING:

....

....

....

*Holy, holy, holy, Lord God Almighty,
which was, and is, and is to come.*
REVELATION 4:8

DAY 353 Today's Date: _____

📍 MY PRAYER FOR TODAY: ....
....
....

READ:

Obadiah–Jonah;
Revelation 5:6–14;
Proverbs 28:25–28

MY TAKEAWAY FROM TODAY'S BIBLE READING:
....
....
....

He that trusteth in his own heart is a fool:
but whoso walketh wisely, he shall be delivered.
PROVERBS 28:26

DAY 354 Today's Date: _____

📍 MY PRAYER FOR TODAY: ....
....
....

MY TAKEAWAY FROM TODAY'S BIBLE READING:
....
....
....

READ:

Micah 1:1–4:5;
Revelation 6:1–7:8;
Proverbs 29:1–8

But they shall sit every man under his vine and
under his fig tree; and none shall make them afraid:
for the mouth of the LORD of hosts hath spoken it.
MICAH 4:4

Today's Date: _____

MY PRAYER FOR TODAY: ....
....
....

MY TAKEAWAY FROM TODAY'S BIBLE READING:
....
....
....

READ:

Micah 4:6–7:20;
Revelation 7:9–8:13;
Proverbs 29:9–14

What doth the LORD require of thee, but to do justly,
and to love mercy, and to walk humbly with thy God?
MICAH 6:8

Today's Date: _____

MY PRAYER FOR TODAY: ....
....
....

READ:

Nahum;
Revelation 9–10;
Proverbs 29:15–23

MY TAKEAWAY FROM TODAY'S BIBLE READING:
....
....
....

The LORD is good, a strong hold in the day of trouble;
and he knoweth them that trust in him.
NAHUM 1:7

DAY 357   Today's Date: _____

📍 **MY PRAYER FOR TODAY:** ....

....

....

READ:

Habakkuk;
Revelation 11;
Proverbs 29:24–27

MY TAKEAWAY FROM TODAY'S BIBLE READING:

....

....

....

*Yet I will rejoice in the LORD,
I will joy in the God of my salvation.*
Habakkuk 3:18

DAY 358   Today's Date: _____

📍 **MY PRAYER FOR TODAY:** ....

....

....

MY TAKEAWAY FROM TODAY'S BIBLE READING:

READ:

Zephaniah;
Revelation 12;
Proverbs 30:1–6

....

....

....

*The LORD thy God in the midst of thee is mighty;
he will save, he will rejoice over thee with joy; he will
rest in his love, he will joy over thee with singing.*
Zephaniah 3:17

Today's Date: _____   **DAY 359**

📍 MY PRAYER FOR TODAY: ....
....
....

MY TAKEAWAY FROM TODAY'S BIBLE READING:

....   **READ:**
....   HAGGAI;
....   REVELATION
....   13:1–14:13;
                                                                                  PROVERBS 30:7–16

Two things have I required of thee; deny me them not before
I die: remove far from me vanity and lies: give me neither
poverty nor riches; feed me with food convenient for me.
PROVERBS 30:7–8

Today's Date: _____   **DAY 360**

📍 MY PRAYER FOR TODAY: ....
....
....

READ: MY TAKEAWAY FROM TODAY'S BIBLE READING:

ZECHARIAH 1–4;   ....
REVELATION   ....
14:14–16:3;   ....
PROVERBS 30:17–20

Not by might, nor by power, but by
my spirit, saith the LORD of hosts.
ZECHARIAH 4:6

DAY 361   Today's Date: _____

📍 MY PRAYER FOR TODAY: ....
....
....

READ:

Zechariah 5–8;
Revelation 16:4–21;
Proverbs 30:21–28

MY TAKEAWAY FROM TODAY'S BIBLE READING:
....
....
....

These are the things that ye shall do; speak ye every man the truth to his neighbour; execute the judgment of truth and peace in your gates.
Zechariah 8:16

DAY 362   Today's Date: _____

📍 MY PRAYER FOR TODAY: ....
....
....

MY TAKEAWAY FROM TODAY'S BIBLE READING:
....
....
....

READ:

Zechariah 9–11;
Revelation 17:1–18:8;
Proverbs 30:29–33

He is Lord of lords, and King of kings: and they that are with him are called, and chosen, and faithful.
Revelation 17:14

Today's Date: _____ **DAY 363**

📍 MY PRAYER FOR TODAY: ....
....
....

MY TAKEAWAY FROM TODAY'S BIBLE READING:
....
....
....

READ:

Zechariah 12–14;
Revelation 18:9–24;
Proverbs 31:1–9

Open thy mouth for the dumb in the cause of all such as are appointed to destruction. Open thy mouth, judge righteously, and plead the cause of the poor and needy.
Proverbs 31:8–9

Today's Date: _____ **DAY 364**

📍 MY PRAYER FOR TODAY: ....
....
....

READ:

Malachi 1–2;
Revelation 19–20;
Proverbs 31:10–17

MY TAKEAWAY FROM TODAY'S BIBLE READING:
....
....
....

His name is called The Word of God. And the armies which were in heaven followed him upon white horses, clothed in fine linen, white and clean.
Revelation 19:13–14

DAY 365　Today's Date: _____

MY PRAYER FOR TODAY: ....

....

....

READ:

Malachi 3–4;
Revelation 21–22;
Proverbs 31:18–31

MY TAKEAWAY FROM TODAY'S BIBLE READING:

....

....

....

And God shall wipe away all tears from their eyes; and there shall be no more death, neither sorrow, nor crying, neither shall there be any more pain: for the former things are passed away.
REVELATION 21:4

THE PRAYER MAP. . .
FOR THE WHOLE FAMILY

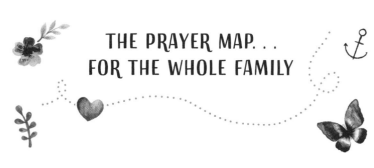

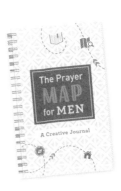

The Prayer Map for Men
978-1-64352-438-2

The Prayer Map for Women
978-1-68322-557-7

The Prayer Map for Girls
978-1-68322-559-1

The Prayer Map for Boys
978-1-68322-558-4

The Prayer Map for Teens
978-1-68322-556-0

This series of purposeful prayer journals is a fun and
creative way to more fully experience the power of
prayer! Each inspiring journal page guides you to
write out thoughts, ideas, and lists. . .which then creates
a specific "map" for you to follow as you talk to God.
Spiral Bound / $7.99